W9-BSP-790

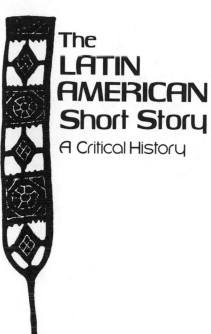

The
LATIN
AMERICAN
Short Story
A Critical History

Twayne's Critical History of the Short Story

William Peden, General Editor
University of Missouri-Columbia

The American Short Story, 1850–1900
J. Donald Crowley, University of Missouri, Columbia

The American Short Story, 1900–1945
Philip Stevick, Temple University

The American Short Story, 1945–1980
Gordon Weaver, University of Oklahoma

The British Short Story, 1890–1945
Joseph M. Flora, University of North Carolina, Chapel Hill

The British Short Story, 1945–1980
Denis Vannatta, University of Arkansas, Little Rock

The Irish Short Story
James Kilroy, Vanderbilt University

The Latin American Short Story
Margaret Sayers Peden, University of Missouri, Columbia

The
LATIN
AMERICAN
Short Story
A Critical History

Margaret Sayers Peden, Editor
University of Missouri-Columbia

Twayne Publishers

The Latin American Short Story
Twayne's Critical History of the
Short Story

Copyright © 1983 by G. K. Hall & Co.

Published in 1983 by Twayne Publishers,
A Division of G. K. Hall & Co.
70 Lincoln Street, Boston, Mass. 02111

Printed on permanent/durable
acid-free paper and bound in
the United States of America

First Printing

Book design and production by
Barbara Anderson

Typeset in 10 pt. Optima by Compset, Inc.,
with display type provided by
County Photo Composition.
Textile design from the
Dover Pictorial Archive Series.

Library of Congress Cataloging in Publication Data

Main entry under title:

The Latin American short story.

   (Twayne's critical history of the modern short story)
   Bibliography: p. 142
   Includes index.
   1. Short stories, Latin American—History and
criticism. 2. Latin American fiction—19th century—
History and criticism. 3. Latin American fiction—20th
century—History and criticism. I. Peden, Margaret
Sayers. II. Series.
PQ7082.S5L35 1983   863'.01'098   83-20
ISBN 0-8057-9351-8

FOR W.H.P.: G.H.B.

*Preparation of this book
was supported by the
Graduate Research Council
of the University of Missouri, Columbia*

Contents

Chronology

1492 October 12, Christopher Columbus lands on one of the Bahama Islands, now known as San Salvador.

1500 Discovery of Brazil by Pedro Alvares Cabral; original names for the territory are Santa Cruz and Ilha de Vera Cruz (Island of the True Cross).

1519 Hernán Cortés arrives in the Aztec city of Tenochtitlan, where a superstitious Moctezuma receives him as a descendant of the god Quetzalcoatl.

1531–1535 Francisco Pizarro conquers the Incan civilization of the Andean mountains, centered in Cuzco.

1609 *Comentarios reales de los Incas* (Royal Commentaries of the Incas) written by the half-Inca, half-Spanish Garsilaso de la Vega, the first truly American writer.

1636 Juan Rodríguez Freile writes *El Carnero* (The Ram) in Colombia. Historical essay with local oral tradition.

1691 Sor Juana Inés de la Cruz, the genius of Latin American baroque, signs her autobiographical "Respuesta a Sor Filotea" (Response to Sor Filotea).

1773 *El lazarillo de los ciegos caminantes entre Buenos Aires y Lima* (El Lazarillo: A Guide of the Inexperienced Travelers between Buenos Aires and Lima), a collection of anecdotal material by Alonso Carrió de la Vandera (known as Concolorvo).

1810–1812 Many Latin American countries declare their independence from Spain. The resulting period of confusion proves unpropitious for the development of literary prose.

1815 Brazil is named a kingdom coequal with Portugal.

1816 José Joaquin Fernández de Lizardi's *El periquillo sarniento* (The Itching Parrot), a fully elaborated novel.

1822 The independence of Brazil is declared by Prince Dom Pedro, who becomes Emperor Pedro I.

1830 French romanticism begins to infiltrate Latin American literature through travelers returning from Paris.

1836 *O cronista* (The Chronicler) is first published, a Brazilian newspaper that includes the first short stories signed by its founders, Justianiano José da Rocha, and others.

1838 The Argentine Esteban Echeverría's "El Matadero" (The Slaughtering Grounds) is the first short fiction in Spanish America.

1839 Birth of Joaquim Maria Machado de Assis, the Cervantes of Brazilian literature, founder of the Brazilian Academy of Letters, and the most important name in Brazilian fiction.

1872ff. Ricardo Palma, born 1833 in Peru, composes *tradiciones* all his adult life.

1870 Publication in Brazil of the First Republican Manifesto; publication of Machado de Assis's *Contos fluminenses* (Rio de Janeiro Stories).

1883 Manuel Gutiérrez Nájera, Mexico, publishes the collection *Cuentos frágiles* (Fragile Stories).

1880s Ecuadorean Juan Montalvo writes *Capítulos que se le olvidaron a Cervantes* (Chapters Cervantes Forgot). The Cuban José Martí produces his remarkable journalistic essays, combining reportage, cultural criticism, and renovated, direct, literary Spanish.

1888 The Nicaraguan-born Rubén Darío publishes his experimental *Azul . . .* (Azure . . .), marking the beginnings of Spanish American modernism.

1888–1891 The prolific Mexican writer Manuel Payno publishes series *Los bandidos de Río Frío* (The bandits of Río Frío).

1895 José Martí and Gutiérrez Nájera die. Rubén Darío and Leopoldo Lugones dominate the Buenos Aires literary community.

1896 Machado de Assis founds the Academia Brasileira de Letras, the Brazilian Academy of Letters.

1898 Gutiérrez Nájera's *Cuentos color de humo* (Smoke-colored stories) is published posthumously. Spain grants Cuba independence, the last stronghold in the American hemisphere of once-powerful Spanish rule.

1899 Birth of Jorge Luis Borges, foremost figure of the Latin American short story.

1904 Baldomero Lillo's *Sub terra: cuadros mineros* (Scenes of mining life) appears in Chile.

1906 Leopoldo Lugones publishes *Las fuerzas extrañas* (Strange Forces).

1910 Lugones is organizer of the cultural arm of the 1910 Centennial. Darío participates with celebratory verse. Publication of "Tuércele el cuello al cisne" (Wring the Swan's Neck) by Enrique González Martínez. Artifically, but conveniently, heralded as the "death" of Spanish American modernism.

1910–1920 Decade of the Mexican Revolution. This period gives rise to a vigorous non-European literature throughout Spanish America, focusing on the poor, peasant, Indian, and black.

1917 Publication of Horacio Quiroga's *Cuentos de amor, de locura y de muerte* (Stories of Love, Madness, and Death), Quiroga's best-known collection and a landmark in Spanish American short story.

1918 *Urupês* (Bracket Fungus), the first major example of twentieth-century short fiction in Brazil, published by the social reformer José Bento Monteiro Lobato. The Chilean poet Vicente Huidobro propounds his esthetic of *creacionismo*, which in later years he will claim is the forerunner of surrealism.

1919 Leopoldo Lugones publishes *Los caballos de Abdera* (The Horses of Abdera).

1920 The Peruvian Enrique López Albújar publishes *Cuentos andinos* (Andean Stories).

1922 The Semana de Arte Moderna (Modern Art Week) in São Paulo inaugurates literary and artistic modernism in Brazil and contemporary vanguard culture.

1926 *Cuentos para una inglesa desesperada* (Stories for a Forlorn English Lady), by Eduardo Mallea, one of Argentina's foremost representatives of existential themes.

1929 *Lenita*, the first novel to be published by Jorge Amado, the most famous living fiction writer in Brazil.

1934 Mário de Andrade, one of the leading figures of Brazilian modernism, publishes *Os contos de Belazarte* (Stories of Belazarte), reflecting his attempt to compose fiction based on Portuguese spoken in Brazil.

1935 *La última niebla* (Last Mist), an early collection of short stories by one of Spanish America's most important women writers, María Luisa Bombal, who after 1944 lived many years in New York.

1936–1939 Period of the Spanish Civil War, which has a profound effect on many Latin American writers, most notably, her poets.

1937 Getúlio Vargas becomes dictator-president of the authoritarian Estado Novo (New State), Brazil's version of fascism. A despondent, erratic, ill Horacio Quiroga commits suicide.

1939–1945 The Second World War isolates South and Central America from Europe economically and culturally. Many trace cultural contemporaneity of this part of the world to the period following the end of the war.

1940 Puerto Rico's literary generation of 1940, including René Márques, Pedro Juan Soto, Emilio Díaz Valcárcel, José Luis González, and Luis Rafael Sánchez.

1944 Publication of *Ficciones,* (Fictions) perhaps still the most widely known collection by Jorge Luis Borges.

1945 The Nobel Prize for literature is awarded to Gabriela Mistral, Chilean poet, the first Latin American to be so honored. A military coup removes Vargas from office in Brazil, and democratic government is restored.

1946 João Guimarães Rosa's *Sagarana* (Collection of Sagas) is published, an early example of his fiction of magical realism.

1950 Peru's literary generation of the 1950s, including Enrique Congrains Martín, Carlos Zavaleta, and Sebastián Salazar Bondy.

1951 Publication of *Un sueño realizado* (A Dream Come True) by Juan Carlos Onetti, an innovator slow to receive appropriate recognition. *Bestiario* (Bestiary) a fantasy collection by the Argentine Julio Cortázar, after Borges the most famous contemporary Latin American *cuentista*.

1952 *Confabulario total* (Confabulario and other inventions), a collection of fantastic tales by the Mexican Juan José Arreola.

1953 *El llano en llamas* (The Flaming Plain), short stories by the Mexican Juan Rulfo, acknowledged as a master for this collection, and the novel *Pedro Páramo* (1955). Publication of *Los pasos perdidos* (The Lost Steps), the most typical early example of Spanish American magical realism.

1954 *Los días enmascarados* (The Masked Days), short stories by Carlos Fuentes, a Mexican writer to become best known for his novels.

1955 Following the overthrow of the Peron dictatorship in Argentina, Borges is named Director of the National Library in Buenos Aires.

1956 One of Cortázar's most widely distributed collection of stories, *Final del juego* (End of the Game).

1960 *Life en español* short story contest elicits submission of 3149 original manuscripts. The existential and protofeminist stories of Clarice Lispector's *Laços de família* (Family ties). Cuban generation of 1960, including Norberto Fuentes, Jesús Díaz Rodríguez, Eduardo Heras León, and Juan Luis Herrero.

1961 Borges shares with Samuel Beckett the International Publishers Formentor Prize.

1962 Translation into English of Borges's *Ficciones,* opening the decade of the boom in Latin American literature in English translation. Gabriel García Márquez, probably the Latin American prose writer most widely read in English, publishes the stories of *Los funerales de la Mamá Grande* (in English, included in *No One Writes to the Colonel and Other Stories*).

1964–1970 *La onda,* (the wave), movement of young Mexican writers, including José Agustín, Gustavo Sainz, Juan Tovar, and René Avilés Fabila.

1964 The government of Jõa Goulart, amid widespread fears of its leftist policies, is deposed by the military in Brazil; intense violence and abridgment of civil liberties and human rights ensue.

1965 *Los mejores cuentos de José Donoso* (The Best Short Stories of José Donoso) a Chilean writer; most of the stories are included in *Charleston & Other Stories*.

1967 Miguel Angel Asturias, Guatemalan novelist and short-story writer noted for his mythic and political writing, is awarded the Nobel Prize for literature.

1970 *The Cardinal Points of Borges* is a special issue of *Books Abroad* in book form, dedicated to Jorge Luis Borges. Salvador Allende is Chile's first democratically elected marxist president.

1971 *Nueva Narrativa Hispanoamericana,* special issue dedicated to the short story. Pablo Neruda, Latin America's most widely translated poet, wins the Nobel Prize for literature. *Review* runs special supplement on the writing of Gabriel García Márquez. *Studies in Short Fiction* dedicated to the Latin American short story.

1972 Winter issue of *Review* focuses on Julio Cortázar. Fall issue of *Review* focuses on José Donoso.

1973 In Chile, a counter-coup of the military deposes Allende government; Allende dies of suicide, or murder. *Modern Fiction Studies 19* dedicated to Borges. *Revista Iberoamericana 39* dedicated to Cortázar.

1974 Ernesto Geisel assumes presidency in Brazil as first elected president since the 1964 coup.

1976 *Books Abroad 50* dedicated to Julio Cortázar.

1977 *Revista Iberoamericana 43* dedicated to Borges.

1980 *Jaula de palabras* (Cage of words), an anthology of fifty-three Mexican short stories edited by Gustavo Sainz. *Review 27* dedicated to contemporary Chilean literature. *Agua quemada* (Burnt Water), latest collection by Carlos Fuentes. (The stories under this title in English are accompanied by a number from previous collections.)

Introduction

The twenty-one Spanish and Portuguese-speaking countries of Latin America have produced an enormous body of short stories and a number of superb creators of brief fiction, among them, Horacio Quiroga, Julio Cortázar, João Guimarães Rosa, Rubén Darío, Gabriel García Márquez, Juan Rulfo, Machado de Assis, and Jorge Luis Borges (Brazil, of course, is the only Latin American country whose language is Portuguese, but its literary production nearly equals that of the Spanish language countries). Of these, probably the only figure widely recognized in the United States for his short fiction is Borges. Why is the English-language-reading public so little familiar with the work of literally scores of Latin American short story writers? To some degree, the answer may lie in the comparative lack of attention devoted to the form in general in the United States. The principal reasons, however, are undoubtedly more direct. North Americans have been slow to recognize Latin American literature. It is only since the "discovery" of Jorge Luis Borges in the early 1960s, and with the explosion in that decade of the novelists of the Boom—García Márquez, Cortázar, Carlos Fuentes, Mario Vargas Llosa, and others—that we seemed to realize there was a literature in the vast lands to our south. Slowly, we are beginning to read Latin American poets, although among many gifted figures I suspect that only the name of Pablo Neruda is familiar to the average well-read North American. It goes without saying that language is the principal barrier to our awareness of the Latin American short story. While ideally those tales, stories, and *ficciones* should be read in the language in which they were written, a number of anthologies and an occasional collection of the works of a single author are beginning to appear in English translation. There are, of course, specialists in the short story among scholars of Latin American literature, including Seymour Menton, Luis Leal, and Enrique Pupo-Walker; as Pupo-Walker has noted, the "amazing success achieved by the Hispanic narrative has resulted in an avalanche of commentaries." In spite of scholarly interest, however, English-language criticism, histories of the genre, and special issues of journals dedicated to the form have been rare. It is to be hoped that the essays in this volume will contribute to the reversal of that trend, and that through them new North American readers will be introduced to a large, varied, and significant body of literature, and that those students already familiar with the writers included here will form additional insights and gain new appreciations of this major Latin American genre.

The appearance of the short story in Latin America closely parallels that of the modern short story in North America. Its influences were largely European (even Poe reached Latin America by way of France) during the nineteenth and early twentieth centuries, although nineteenth-century styles arrived somewhat later and lingered somewhat longer in Latin America than the corresponding movements in Europe. With the advent of modernism—and Latin America had its own versions of this larger phenomenon—Latin American short-story writers began to speak with more authentically indigenous voices. The forms of their fiction, its themes, its modes, became so diverse that since the decade of the 1920s it has been virtually impossible to speak of sharply defined broad movements; rather, there have been regional clusters of authors, loosely knit schools, and individual writers who composed narratives that somehow fit within the genre defined as brief fiction.

Latin America's literatures have traditionally been linked to those of Europe. Its earliest landmarks are the chronicles, those letters and reports sent back to Spain and Portugal by awed, if determined, seekers after gold and souls, the explorers and priests—often one and the same—who relayed to the Old World the real and exaggerated glories of the New. The contemporary novelist and short-story writer Carlos Fuentes has divided the literature of the New World into three periods: the utopian, the epic, and the mythic. The utopian period in Fuentes's classification represents the comparatively brief years of exploration and discovery. Some writers have hazarded that if the New World had not existed, it would, out of Europe's need for it, have been invented; and for a while, this great new continent seemed to promise the opportunities Sir Thomas More had envisioned. The search for Utopia rather quickly evolved into a period that lasted for several centuries, the epic conquest, the colonization, expansion, population, and development of the vast spaces of South and Central America, and Mexico, and even, we should remember, southern and western United States. (The mythic literature Fuentes defines is offered as the only solution to exhausted epic modes, and its ambience has in recent years given rise to a manner-of-telling referred to as magical realism.) During the long epic process, Latin America was very directly—economically, politically, socially, and literarily—bound to the mother continent. Even as the decadence of Spain and Portugal set in so rapidly on the heels of the conquest, its commanding literary figures dominated seventeenth-century literature in the New World. This European literature realized its culmination as its influence reached the shores of the new continents, which has led to the assessment, and the bizarre conclusion, that the true beginnings of Latin American literature were formed in the last convulsions of an exhausted European baroque expression.

As the world powers of Spain and Portugal declined, Latin America, during a primarily dormant eighteenth century, gradually turned for inspiration to a sister Latin nation, France. During the early years of the nineteenth century, Latin Americans eagerly absorbed French revolutionary ideas. In the political sphere, such influence may be seen as early as 1811 in Paraguay's independence, in 1816 with the declaration of independence from Spain of the United Provinces of La Plata (the southern cone of South America), and in 1922 with Brazilian independence from Portugal, soon to be followed by similar actions throughout the continent. These wars for independence from the mother countries were echoed in the literary rebellion of romanticism, imported directly from France and first observable in narrative in the Argentine and Colombian novels of Jorge Isaacs and José Mármol.

There is general agreement that the Latin American short story was born during this romantic period with the publication of "El matadero" (The slaughtering grounds) by the socially and politically oriented Argentine Esteban Echeverría. As Naomi Lindstrom describes, one may argue that certain fragments from previously published longer narratives bear certain characteristics of and similarities with the short story, but even though "El matadero" does not conform to current definitions of the genre, its composition in the late 1830s is a landmark in the history of short fiction in Spanish. Although its subject matter is searingly realistic, it is clear that it was published during the full flower of romantic influence. In Brazil, David Foster places the initiation of the form at a later date, the 1870s during the second generation of romantics.

Romanticism was a long-lived movement in Latin America, spanning the decades of earliest influence in southern South America, the 1830s and 1840s, and lasting well into the 1860s and 1870s in some countries and with some writers. Realism and naturalism, whose effect was most strongly felt during the last three decades of the nineteenth century, followed in rapid order, coexisting with the last bastions of romanticism, and often mixed indiscriminately in the same works with romanticism. It is difficult to find in Latin America examples of pure naturalist work; realism was adapted somewhat more effectively, although in these works as well one can often identify sections of high romantic prose, especially in descriptions of nature. It must be stressed that although this schema of European influences is in general accurate, a number of factors makes suspect any absolute correlation between European and American movements. Certain exclusively American realities were not to be denied even in the midst of styles decreed by models from across the seas. Gaucho and Indian cultures, undeniably American social and political truths, branded Latin American literature with their distinctive marks. Some American writers had also assimilated a particularly Spanish brand of romanticism called *costumbrismo*, the depiction of local manners and scenes, and, as in the case of the Peruvian Ricardo Palma, invented their own forms, in his case neither fiction nor fact, but a whimsical blend incorporating local color and folklore. It was, nevertheless, European models who set the stage for the ensuing literary development that was to be considered Latin America's first indigenous movement.

Modernismo, as it is now defined, had its beginnings about 1888 and survived as a fairly cohesive movement for some two decades. Many of its characteristics were absorbed from the traditional French sources: the cold measuring eye, the visual perfection of the parnassians; the musical sonority and symbolic vocabulary of the symbolists. *Modernismo* represented an elitist, art-for-art's-sake accord that swept the Spanish American world, and it is a matter of pride that with *modernismo* the traditional direction of literary influences was temporarily reversed: briefly, Spanish America shaped literary tastes in Spain.

Modernismo was primarily a movement of poets. Rubén Darío was its principal exponent, the magnetic figure who gave coherence to the movement. This supremely poetic phenomenon produced few prose works, and though a few of Latin America's most important short-story writers were formed by *modernismo*—Horacio Quiroga, Leopoldo Lugones, Darío himself—only in an occasional story such as "La Muerte de la emperatriz de China" (the Death of the Empress of China) do story and form seem to coalesce.

With the modernist movements, the literary histories of Brazil and Spanish America, until that time roughly parallel, began to diverge. Brazilian *modernismo* is more closely allied to the vanguardist movements of the 1920s than to the Spanish American movement whose name it shares, and was emerging at about the time the latter was beginning to ebb. Unlike the earlier Spanish-language version, Brazilian *modernismo* had its origins in the plastic arts, specifically in a 1916 exhibition in São Paulo of German and expressionist and cubist painters. In 1922 this São Paulo group, which included a number of literary figures, sponsored with a similar group from Rio de Janeiro a Modern Art Week in São Paulo; the resulting artistic experimentation soon spread across Brazil. This movement may be less cohesive than its Spanish-language counterpart, and fairly rapidly split into subgroups such as the *antropofagistas* ("cannibals") and the *verdeamarelistas* ("green-yellows," a name derived from the colors of the Brazilian flag). As David Foster points out, this movement, whose members comprise the Generation of 1922, dominated the literary scene in Brazil for some fifty years, culminating in the figure of João Guimarães Rosa.

Similarly, Spanish American literature dating from the end of the modernist period (which is often cited as 1910, but in fact continued for many years after that date) is marked by few definable groups or movements, rather, by continuing waves of conservatism and experimentation.

Horacio Quiroga was the first truly major Spanish American short-story writer. With his first collection of stories in 1917 his position as a premier *cuentista* was established. As John Brushwood notes, Quiroga was the first Spanish American to devote his attention to theory, and his "Decalogue of the Perfect Short Story Writer" today offers interesting insights into his esthetic. As Quiroga was creating his haunted, obsessive tales in Uruguay, conflicting literary currents were swirling across Spanish America. Mexico was suffering the trauma of its Revolution, and the Indian and the *mestizo* became the focus of its art and of its literature as well. This passionately nationalist art was soon to be followed by the cosmopolitan and experimental works of the *contemporáneos* of the 1930s. In fact, during the 1930s vanguardist movements flourished in all of Spanish America, echoing Brazilian *modernismo,* and once again European trends were eagerly sought after. Surrealism inspired a multitude of Spanish American *"ismos"*: *cubismo, creacionismo, ultraísmo,* and *estridentismo,* among others. Contemporary with these universalist trends was the nativist focus of what was perhaps in broadest terms the dominant mood of the 1930s, *criollismo*. A *criollo* was American-born, and the writing consistent with this epithet turned its eyes inward, toward the land and its inhabitants. The result was literature of self-examination and self-identification. The conflicts that Domingo Faustino Sarmiento had posed in 1845 in his essay *Civilización i barbarie* (Civilization and Barbarism) were explored anew through the old polarities of the provincial and the urban, conservatism and progress. The lives of the citizens of South America's great cities were examined in the brilliant, unflattering light of their own social castes, as well as contrasted with the peoples of the vast open spaces of the continent. During the period between the two great wars, as it sought to define its own realities, Latin America shook off and simultaneously absorbed the literary modes of Europe, and for the first time, the great writers of the English language, foremost among them, James Joyce.

By the 1940s Latin America's literatures blended synchronically with world literature. Particularly in southern South America, which was most closely allied with European cultural models, writers delved into the psychological narrative and exhibited the neuroses of European angst. The 1950s and 1960s produced the experimental story, interior monologue, stream of consciousness, new departures in form, the narrative as prose poem, and typographical experimentation. It was during this period that the reputation of Jorge Luis Borges, Latin America's giant among short-story writers, was established. With the 1960s the English-language literary community began to acknowledge the presence of a literature that in fact burst upon them in the form of the Boom. Simultaneously, magical realism, a term imperfectly defined, often controversial, but perhaps Latin America's most authentic literary mode, came into vogue.

The phenomenon of the Boom is due in large part to the "discovery" of Borges by the French in 1961, when he shared the International Publishers Formentor Prize with Samuel Beckett. Following that award, Borges's stories began to appear in English translation, opening the floodgates to a stream of literature that continues unabated until today. Borges changed the shape of literature, and made common a term of his invention—the *ficción*.

The third great *cuentista* of Latin America, sharing that distinction with Borges and Horacio Quiroga, is the Argentine Julio Cortázar, whom George McMurray accurately describes as a seeker after the surrealist absolute. Of a number of internationally recognized writers such as Alejo Carpentier, Jorge Amado, Pablo Neruda, Gabriel García Márquez, Carlos Fuentes, Mario Vargas Llosa, João Guimarães Rosa, César Vallejo, Ernesto Sábato, Octavio Paz, Guillermo Cabrera Infante, Juan Rulfo, José Donoso, Osman Lins, José Agustín, Clarice Lispector, Demetrio Aguilera Malta, and a host of lesser recognized younger writers, Cortázar is the most consistently and most essentially a short-story writer.

Since the 1960s Latin America can truly be said to have influenced world literature, and its writers have been recognized as masters of the short story and other genres as well. Although magical realism, a uniquely American movement, typifies the work of many of the authors contained in this study, even it cannot be said to characterize all of Latin American literature. No one manner of telling can satisfactorily define the variety of literatures of Latin America's many nations or its historical periods. Because of the number of countries and races and cultures that have shaped it, the diversity of the Latin American short story is probably unsurpassed.

If a single presence can be identified in such diversity it is that of the hovering figure of Edgar Allan Poe, whose long shadow spreads across the history of the genre in Spanish America, though less perceptibly in Brazil. In his "Decalogue," Horacio Quiroga listed Poe first among his masters, and some of his early stories are transparent recreations of Poe's. With Borges, one again finds Poe's influence in the predominance of the detective story pattern; through much of his intellectual brilliance shines the game of the puzzle, the search, the occult solution. It is significant that the third of the triumvirate, Julio Cortázar, translated into Spanish all of Poe's prose works and frequently refers to Poe in his critical writings on the genre.

Latin America has been extremely receptive to the short story. The essays that follow chart the main currents and the principal figures of the historical mainstream of the Latin American short story, suggesting the outlines of the great depth and breadth of the genre in these lands.

Margaret Sayers Peden

University of Missouri, Columbia

MAJOR FIGURES
IN THE BRAZILIAN
SHORT STORY

David William Foster

The short story has existed in one form or another in Brazil since virtually the beginning of Brazilian literature during the colonial period, although its major manifestations may be dated from the nineteenth century, originally with romanticism and then in one of its finest forms, in the fiction of Joaquim Maria Machado de Assis. As elsewhere in Latin America and in Western literature in general, the Brazilian short story is a protean form, which on one end of the literary spectrum impinges on journalism (the tradition of the *cronicas*—literally, chronicles—which are more vignettes of local color, customs, and national foibles than they are narrative fictions) and on the other end overlaps with the evocative prose poem (e.g., the microtexts of Dalton Trevisan discussed below).

The quantity of short stories produced in Brazil since the end of the nineteenth century is staggering, so much so that it is the only Brazilian literary genre to which an entire bibliographic register has been devoted (two volumes list no fewer than 2,987 collections.) Although many of these publications are of only historical value, the number of major names is such that this chapter can do no more than suggest the wealth of material and the intense sophistication of the genre in Brazil. To demonstrate adequately the artistic accomplishments of the authors, this presentation focuses in some detail on individual works from representative collections of landmark authors, two from the nineteenth century and the rest from the twentieth century. This means that very

1

few works can be analyzed in the space available, but these discussions should provide an image of the material sufficient to suggest the extent of works available for subsequent study.

Critical Realism

Although Brazil had a flourishing literary tradition during the colonial period and on into the nineteenth century, it is inevitable that modern Brazilian literature be dated from the 1870s when Joaquim Maria Machado de Assis (1839–1908) was in his prime as a writer.

One general limitation of Latin American literature before the mid-twentieth century is the general reliance by writers on European literary models, a dependency that resulted in a considerable amount of derivative production. Few writers were able to go beyond their models to produce original variations, and those who insisted on ignoring the prestigious trends of French and British literature paid the price of exclusion from the academies and literary supplements. (It was not until José Hernández's Gaucho's epic, *Martín Fierro* [1872], became such a monument of Argentine popular culture that it could no longer be ignored that that nation's literary establishment began to pay attention to the non-mainline literature the work exemplified.)

The importance of Machado in this context is that he was virtually the only novelist of nineteenth-century Latin America to attain a significant assimilation of European literary models and to produce a body of writings that are every bit the equal of the great French and British leaders. Indeed, when examined alongside Machado's realist accomplishments, the canon of the novel in Latin America in the nineteenth-century is unimpressive indeed, although it is incontestable that some of these works demand reevaluation for other than their adherence to the models chosen by Machado.

Machado's fiction is outstanding for two basic reasons: (1) its intensely ironic scrutiny of the pretensions of the dominant bourgeois society, and (2) its expression of the ambiguity of the texture of human existence. While Brazil is an ethnically complex society, the nineteenth century saw the rapid emergence, abetted to a great degree by the period of empire that bridged colonial rule and republican independence, of a middle class that sought to impose its values as the social and cultural norm of the country. Thus the complex fabric of a society with many conflicting cultural traditions was overlaid by a pattern of social norms that strove, and continues to strive, for a homogeneity of conduct and values derived from prevailing European middle-class culture. The results are mainly seen by contemporary writers as ludicrous, pathetic, and often tragic. For Machado, the distance between the ideal and the entire range of human and social phenomena that lay outside the bourgeois model could only be treated through ironic discourse, which would compare the facade of social unity with forces that implicitly challenged the ideal by failing to conform to its version of human nature and society.

One of the facets of human nature that bourgeois norms cannot address to any adequate degree is the essential ambiguity of existence, the simple fact that human behavior (as Freud, whom Machado significantly foreshadowed, was to reveal) is torn by drives and impulses that do not fit rational schemes. Moreover, the complexity of human life is such that much of what we do and experience simply does not yield to any attempt to interpret it. Thus narrative fiction becomes the creation of models who, rather than explaining or interpreting, present events with appropriate highlighting of their internal contradictions. In such a vision of human experience there is an excess of event and a deficiency of exegesis, and this accounts both for the complexity of Machado's works and their interest to contemporary readers for whom literature is not facile reductionist interpretation of the grain of human life.

In addition to his prodigious accomplishments in the realm of the realist-psychological novel, Machado may be identified as virtually the initiator of the short story in Brazil, and he is often called the Cervantes of Brazilian letters. The story "Singular Occorrência" (18??; "Singular Occurrence")[1] has been analyzed as a "metatext not only of Machado's concern with the ambiguities of the human experience that polite society cannot account for in terms of its own ideological construction of the world, but also of his typically nineteenth-century rhetorical strategies for the framing of ambiguous narrative."[2] In the story, the narrator shares with us a singular event, the momentary unfaithfulness of an otherwise exemplary lover. The protagonists and the narrator are unable or unwilling to share with the reader an explanation for this lapse; the impact of the story turns on the mystery of this event, the detail with which it is evoked, and its essential inexplicability. By being unable or refusing to interpret the event, the story contravenes a fundamental storytelling requirement: fulfill the reader's desire to know in exchange for the reader's attention. Contravention of this requirement underscores Machado's position toward the complexity of human experience he is concerned with portraying.

"Missa do galo" (1894; "Midnight Mass") is an excellent example of both Machado's concern for the flow of human emotion beneath the surface of an apparently placid and ordered bourgeois life, and his use of the conceit of a personal narrator who is at a loss to explain the full import of the events he describes. A young man from the provinces is waiting up late one Christmas Eve to go to midnight mass. His reading is interrupted by the sudden and almost phantasmagoric appearance of the woman of the house in her diaphanous wrapper (December is the beginning of summer in Brazil). She initiates with him one of those sexual exchanges in which the directness of unexpressed physical attraction is counterpointed by the banality of words spoken in conversation. Their emotion-charged dialogue is interrupted by the call to mass from which the young narrator returns the next morning, never to see the woman again. At the outset of the story, we have learned from him that she was a passive and distracted sort who had long ago grown resigned to her husband's extramarital adventures. The narrator discloses his provincial naivete by not understanding, when his host announces that he will spend the night at the theater, that this is a euphemism for his lover's chambers. His hostess's mother is quite annoyed at the young man's request to be allowed to go along to what he innocently believes will be a dramatic performance, and the servants giggle at his error.

Thus the story proposes two series of basic oppositions. On the narrative level there is the provincial innocent versus the sophisticated ways of the city, and the host's libertine ways versus his wife's Christian resignation; her normally distracted behavior versus her nervous sensuality during the surprise late-night visit to her guest, and the disjunction between her erratic and seemingly provocative behavior in that encounter and the almost irrational banality of topics of conversation that her interlocutor is at a loss to follow. On the level of the narration there is opposition between the narrator as one who has assumed the responsibility of explaining a curious event and his uncomfortable and bewildered participation in something that he cannot quite piece together.

There is also opposition between the "then" of the event and the "now" of the telling, a separation that customarily exists in stories that relate something that happened in the past. In this case, the difference becomes ironic, for the participant as narrator should presumably be in a position to interpret explicitly such an occurrence. That he does not results in a stance toward the act of storytelling, not in the sense that the event cannot be explained (the contemporary hypothesis of absent meaning), but in the fact that the narrator refuses to do so. Machado's works challenge his readers to draw their own conclusions, and the only ones that would fit the facts presented by his narrators refer to behavior that late nineteenth-century Brazilian victorian society was loath to admit.

In the case of "Missa do galo," set against the backdrop of a religious feast day, the conclusion to be drawn is that model Christian wives could be consumed by irrepressible sexual passion. Machado is too clever to describe any consumation of that passion, for it would have earned his writing swift condemnation as immoral. He does, however, resort to ambiguity in the ironic inability of his narrators to formulate precise interpretations of events. This strategy not only protected him from severe censure, but ensured that his works would have the sense of complex human behavior that has made them such an integral part of Latin American fiction.

Naturalism

Inspired by a form of romantic socialism that was the opposite of the prevailing self-satisfaction of early twentieth-century Brazilian society, José Bento Monteiro Lobato (1882–1948) was a crusading writer in the naturalistic tradition whose work still occupies a very controversial place in that country's literature. The tone of many of his writings alternates between sarcastic humor directed against social and intellectual pretensions, particularly Brazil's desire to be modern, and intense outrage over the oppressive stagnation brought about by the self-congratulatory myths of national importance.

The title piece of the 1918 collection Urupês (Bracket Fungus) is indicative of Lobato's concerns and his narrative strategies. The title refers to a type of fungus, and the stories were received with indignation because of their scathing mockery of unpleasant features of Brazilian national life, foreshadowing to a great degree the strong current of social realism that would emerge in the literature of the 1930's. Lobato is a self-confident, omniscient, and frequently overbearing narrator: his lack of subtlety and the complete absence of anything resembling ambiguity are in marked contrast to Machado de Assis's fiction. Indeed, it is legitimate to question the conventional fictionality of some of Lobato's writings. Often more interested in making an editorial point concerning Brazilian society, his narratives become transparent illustrations with little fictional density. This is the case in "Urupês," where

Lobato is intent on refuting artistic idealizations of the Indian. Several nineteenth-century writers in Brazil, with counterparts elsewhere in Spanish America, had contributed to an image of the New World Indian as an embodiment of Rousseau's noble savage. Particularly noteworthy in this regard were the novels of José de Alencar (1829–1877) like *Iracema* (1865) or *O guaraní* (1857; The Guaraní).

"Urupês" opens with a humorously sarcastic review of indigenous culture in Brazilian literature, with specific reference to the saccharine writings of Alencar (the Indianism movement) and to a new variety of distorted images, caboclism (the *caboclo* is the acculturated Indian). For Lobato, the latter appears to represent indigenous culture in the guise of neoprimitive folklore; in fact, this nativist reworking of the image of the Indian came to constitute one of the major underpinnings of the modernist movement in Brazil. Lobato's text dates from 1918; Mário de Andrade's folklore novel *Macunaíma*, with its cosmic vision of indigenous culture and that culture's mythic value for Brazilian national identity, was published in 1928.

For Lobato, both of these images, one based on the romantic concept of the noble savage and the newer one, in which the Indian has "traded in his feathers for a straw hat," are distortions of the sociocultural facts. To refute these sanitized portraits, Lobato creates a fictional native, Jeca Tatu, whose lifestyle he describes so that his readers will have a true concept of the Indian's situation. Rather than contrasting distorted concepts of the Indian with sociological and anthropological facts, Lobato, through the person of Jeca Tatu, presents an exaggerated and ironic inventory of the reasons why Jeca Tatu is little more than a primitive animal and why his race will never amount to much in the history of Brazilian civilization. Although Lobato invokes all of the racial shibboleths of a bourgeois society convinced that the Indian (and, of course, the black and many immigrant groups) is subhuman, the reader realizes that the author is ridiculing these prejudices: "Poor Jeca Tatu! How beautiful you are in novels and how ugly you are in reality!"

To develop his image of Jeca Tatu, Lobato uses statements that constitute a sort of emphatic rhetorical repetition. Lobato continues this rhetorical device by building a series of descriptions emphasizing common misconceptions. For example, he focuses on a traditional posture of the Indian: he does not stand or sit on the floor or sit on a chair; he squats, and how can an advanced society be possible when one squats? Lobato contrasts the standard features of so-called civilized society with what Jeca Tatu and his family do: "No table settings. Isn't the hand a complete place setting—spoon, fork and knife all in one?" "No closets or trunks. Clothing is stored away on his body. He only has two sets of clothes, the one he is wearing and the one being washed." The strategy of juxtaposing contrasting societal norms, of using rhetorical questions, of exaggerated expressions of surprise that one might expect behavior to be any different among such people, make up the principal stylistic elements that convey Lobato's ridicule of the romantic image of the Indian and acknowledgement of the misery that is his lot in modern Brazil.

Lobato closes his poetic evocation of Jeca Tatu by turning specifically to the tropes of the idealizing novels. After a series of distancing statements such as, "He only sings lugubrious prayers," the narrator repeats one of the standard lyrical evocations of the Brazilian landscape: "In the midst of Brazilian nature, so rich in forms and colors. . . ." This *locus amoenus* is followed by a statement regarding the abyss that separates the Indian from his putative Eden, a couplet that confirms the underlying irony of racial stereotypes:

> Only he does not speak, does not sing, does not
> laugh, does not love.
> Only he, in the midst of so much life, does not
> live. . . .

This work, with its demand that the reader accept the author's refutation of romantic images on the one hand and racial shibboleths on the other, is neither subtle nor complex. It is illustrative of a social commentary significantly different from the equally antibourgeois irony of Machado de Assis.

It is appropriate to mention the fiction of Afonso Henrique de Lima Barreto (1881–1922), a selection of which has only recently been translated into English. Lima Barreto's immediate importance is as a black writer, and critics have noted the early presence of black and mulatto (e.g., Machado de Assis) in Brazilian letters. Yet Lima Barreto was also of considerable significance for his attention to black sociocultural issues, an emphasis notably lacking in the writings of previous authors of the same racial origins. Rather than stressing racial assimilation, Lima Barreto focuses on ethnic differences and, well within the tradition of ironic realism established by Machado, on the complex patterns of prejudice in a society that early gave the impression of being racially and culturally integrated. Of special interest is his concern for the sexual exploitation of nonwhite women, and one of his major novels, the posthumous *Clara dos Anjos* (1923–1924), deals with the seduction and abandonment of the mulatto woman of the title by her social, sexual, and racial "superior," an upperclass white man. The short stories appended to the 1948 publication of this novel in book form (the 1923–1924 publication was serialized in a magazine) include a selection of Lima Barreto's stories denouncing a broad spectrum of Brazilian social vices.

His collection of stories *Histórias e sonhos; contos* (1920; Short Stories and Dreams; Stories) is a prime example of his short fiction, with its emphasis on subjects concerning the life of poor blacks in the Rio suburbs and the incursion of African cultural elements into Brazilian social life (as in the *carnaval*). Although perhaps of greater importance as a novelist and essayist than as a short-story writer, Lima Barreto's work is nevertheless a significant milestone in the development of varieties of social criticism in Brazilian fiction.

Modernism

Mário Raul de Morais Andrade (1893–1945) is one of the most important transition figures in Brazilian literature. His comic novel *Macunaíma* (1928) deals in rabelaisian style with the frustrated attempts of a native chieftain to integrate himself into modern industrial and technological society as represented by São Paulo, the progressive city that hosted the revolutionary Week of Modern Art (1922) that was Brazil's entrance into the postwar international modernist movement. Although of central importance for this novel and for his vanguard poetry—Andrade was one of the principal doctrinal spokesmen for modernism—he also wrote a number of fine stories marked by their attention to colloquial registers (one of the modernist goals was to affirm the presence of a Brazilian national language) and by the irony with which he treated the stuffy conventions of Brazilian middle-class life. Representative of these stories is "O peru de natal" (The Christmas Turkey) from the posthumous *Contos novos* (1956; New Stories) in which the persistent presence of a dour father, for whom the family is still in rigorous mourning, is exorcized by the adolescent narrator's insistence that the family have a turkey with all the trimmings for its quiet, intimate Christmas meal. Through the almost offhand comments of the narrator, we sense the sardonic contrast between the severe paternalism of the absent father and frank and irrepressible pleasure of a feast of which he would never have approved: this is the anthropologic

schism of culture versus nature, repressive conventionalism versus the
gesture (unconscious in the other family members) toward uninhibited
sensualism imposed by the son in defiant repudiation of the domineer-
ing father figure.

Social Realism

Jorge Amado (1912–   ) has recently celebrated the fiftieth anniver-
sary of his career as Brazil's most prolific living author. Indeed, until
recent translations of authors such as João Guimarães Rosa, Amado was
long the only contemporary Brazilian novelist well known by readers in
the United States. Nevertheless, he has not attained the level of integra-
tion into the mainstream of his country's literature that his international
fame would suggest is his due. Many readers consider his works enjoy-
able, with a good sense of Brazilian society, particularly that of his
native Bahia region; however, they do not consider him a sophisticated
or complex writer. In short, his works are eminently "readerly," to use
Roland Barthes's term for works that lend themselves to easy com-
prehension; but they are not particularly "writerly," in the sense of
placing demands on the reader and creating an awareness of the risks
and complexities of literature.

Amado's most recent bestseller, *Farda fardão, camisola de dormir*
(1979; Uniform, Gown, Nightie) is an example of the success as well as
of the limitations noted by critics of his work. The novel deals humorously and satirically with the politics of the Brazilian Academy of Letters
(of which Amado himself is a member). Published at a time when there
has been considerable relaxation of censorship in Brazil, it deals with
his own long-standing commitment to social reform (he has a long
history of persecution at the hands of the moral and political right in
Brazil) and with two unmovable cultural establishments in the country:
the literary corporation and the politically involved military.

Amado is at his best (and at his most exasperating for critics who have
reservations about him as a truly original writer) in his novels. Yet he has
also written short stories that evince his commitment to folkloristic
portraits of segments of Brazilian society that have not often had an
adequate narrative voice. "De como o mulato Porciúncula descarregou
seu defunto" ("How Porciúncula the Mulatto Got the Corpse Off His
Back") from the *Histórias de Bahia* (1963; Bahia Stories) is a fine
example of Amado in full command of his prodigious storytelling talents. It concerns the fate of Maria of the Veil, a young prostitute obsessed

with marriage and the bridal veil. Having been seduced by a general's son, who promised to give her a wedding in order to possess her, she is beaten and thrown out by her father. She makes her way to the port city and becomes a prostitute at Tibéria's whorehouse, where she is pursued unsuccessfully by the mulatto Porciúncula. When she dies of the flu, still a girl, Tibéria and her women fulfill Maria's dying wish: they arrange a mock wedding for her. Dressed in a patchwork veil, Maria's corpse is wedded by Tibéria, who acts the role of priest, to Porciúncula. Thus in death she attains the romantic fantasy denied her in life, and Porciúncula "wins" his woman. Amado's story here reveals the hallmark of his fiction: emphasis on the underlying good nature of the common people, despite the socially terrible lot of their lives. Tibéria is the madam with the heart of gold, Maria is the unsullied innocent, Porciúncula is the faithful "spouse," and the narrative frame is the story told by a good-natured raconteur.

Amado uses a framed text in the sense that one storyteller narrates another's tale. In this case, it is Porciúncula's story of his relationship and "marriage" with Maria. In turn, Maria's personal story is related to Porciúncula by her and also by the madam Tibéria, who fills him in on many of the details the young girl had told her. The result of such extensive framing is immediately clear: a good portion of the story concerns not the actual details of Maria's short life and quick death, but of references to the process of evoking a tale and telling it. The narrator divides his text into two stages. The first is a reference to a gringo who hangs around the Bahia port. He is a fugitive from justice, having killed his lover and another man. The narrator spends some time describing this foreigner and his close-lipped nature. Referring to the secrets (particularly homicidal ones) of one's past (one's personal story) as a corpse, the narrator asserts:

Listen, a corpse is a heavy load, and many's the brave man I've seen who let his load slip into a stranger's hands when booze loosened him up. Let alone two corpses, a man and a woman, with those wounds in the belly. . . . The gringo never let his drop, which was why his ribs were bent, from the weight of it, no doubt. He asked for no one's help, but here and there they told about it in detail, and it turned into a pretty good story, with parts for laughing and parts for crying, the way a good story should be.

By contrast, the chance comment of the gringo in a bar triggers the telling of another story, that of Porciúncula's involvement with Maria of the Veil. In this case the man allows himself to be unburdened of the corpse he bears. It is Porciúncula's own story to tell, but the narrator relates it with appropriate apologies for his less skillful abilities. The implication is that Porciúncula is more important for this skill as a storyteller than for any part he plays in the story he has to relate:

This Porciúncula, he was the best-talking mulatto I ever knew, and that's saying a lot. So literate, so smooth, you'd think, not knowing his background, that he'd worn out a schoolbench though old Ventura hadn't put him into any school but out on the streets and the waterfront. He was such a wizard at telling stories that if this one turns sour in my mouth it's not the fault of the story or of the mulatto Porciúncula.

In conjunction with Amado's implicit belief that life is an ironic story worth the attention of an urbane and subtle raconteur is the image of the storyteller as a student of life. Rather than the product of formal training, he is a "natural literate," trained in the streets and on the waterfronts of hard daily life. It is thus not surprising that the method of telling is as much the subject of the narrator's story as the actual sequence of events that he ostensibly sets out to relate.

The charm of Amado's fiction for many readers derives from a certain practice of softening the harsh circumstances of life to make them more appropriate objects of the urbane teller's art. Stories like that of Maria of the Veil have long been the stuff of an abundant tradition of social denunciation in Latin American literature: the miserable child-prostitute forced into a life of physical and spiritual depravity by a value system that obliges her to be the sacrificial victim of its structure of human exploitation. This is the well-worn theme of Latin American society as a bordello (see Mario Vargas Llosa's novel *La casa verde* (1966; *The Green House*). An alternative, and somewhat more recent, tradition is to portray girls like Maria in grotesquely emblematic terms rather than as sociologic case studies (see Jorge Ibarguengoitia's Mexican police novel *Las muertas* (1977; *The Dead Women*); her story is particularly suited to such treatment because of the black mass denouement in honor of her obsession with the marriage ceremony.

Amado's sanitizing of typical cases like Maria's makes the social reality much less threatening to the reader and much more entertaining. The pattern of opposites we see elsewhere in Amado's fiction is amply evident here as part of the vitiation of any element of horror the story might hold: Maria's rape by the general's son and expulsion by her father is counterbalanced by Porciúncula's natural goodness; the fate of the woman as a child prostitute is assuaged by the motherly attentions

of Tibéria and other members of the household; her early death becomes the occasion for fulfillment of her romantic fantasy; and the
overall dreadfulness of her life is framed lovingly by Porciúncula's
perfect art: "It was here the mulatto Porciúncula stopped, and there was
no getting another word of the story out of him. He's unloaded his
corpse on us, he'd relieved himself of the burden. Mercedes still wanted
to know if the coffin had been white-for-a-virgin or black-for-a-sinner.
Porciúncula shrugged his shoulders and swatted flies."

Thus Amado projects a metafictional image concerning the continuity between life and narrative: life is a story and the participants in
life are natural storytellers who do not invent fictions but who unburden
themselves of their "corpses" by turning their experiences into skillful
tales. This image may have little to do with the actual life as experienced
by individuals who inhabit the social environment re-created in the
story, and even less with the folk narratives the writer attempts to
reconstruct. It is, however, a form of fiction that has won for Amado
considerable stature in contemporary Brazilian literature.

Existentialism

Clarice Lispector's award-winning collection of short stories, Laços de
família (1960; Family Ties) is one of the most important works by a
woman author in Latin American literature, especially because of its
emphasis on the role of women in Western society. Lispector (1925–
1977), although born in the Ukraine, was raised in Brazil. One of a
group of important women authors in her adoptive country, Lispector
belongs to a spectrum of writers in Latin America whose importance has
been enhanced because of their treatment of women's issues: Rosario
Castellanos and Elena Poniatowska in Mexico, Marta Lynch and Sylvina
Bullrich in Argentina, and Marta Brunet and María Luisa Bombal in
Chile are only some of the women who have attracted intensive critical
attention in recent years.

It would be reductive to see Lispector as concerned only with the
oppression of woman in a society that mythifies her. Nevertheless,
Lispector's general concern for the volcanic nature of human personality that is barely contained by the repressive rituals of a well-ordered
society finds its natural corollary in the lot of women who are frustrated
in their attempts to reconcile a drive for existential identity with the
patterns of that society. Brazil, like Argentina and Chile, is a country in

which women moved into the professions long before they did in the United States, and they have long been prominent in the arts in Brazil, quite apart from any drive for sexual recognition. Yet it would be a mistake to believe that because a privileged class of women (typically, those from the professional middle class and their daughters) is well represented in the arts, there is not a significant number still trapped by the myths of the feminine mystique.

It is significant that Lispector, like Marta Lynch in Argentina, does not deal with women's issues in society in general: indeed, there are as yet few prominent women writers in Latin America to address the role of women in a wide variety of socioeconomic sectors. One finds no prominent Latin American equivalent of the Spanish Mercedes Rodo-dera who deals with lower-middle-class women, although the novels of Argentina's Reina Roffé are notable for not emphasizing women of Buenos Aires's leisured class. Like Lynch or Sylvina Bullrich, Lispector focuses on women who, because of their "bird in a gilded cage" status, can afford the luxury of protracted and intensive introspection. Although many of her women are unable to articulate fully any coherent image of themselves and their functions in a specific social structure, they are in a position to spend long hours in self-contemplation before the mirror ("Devaneio e embriaguez duma rapariga") or in wandering around the zoo attempting to establish sympathetic communication with the imprisoned animals ("O búfalo").

In "Devaneio e embriaguez duma rapariga" (1960; "The Daydream of a Drunken Woman") the narrator, who fluctuates between speaking indirectly for the woman and characterizing her by speaking about her, notes: "She looked around her, patient and obedient. Ah, words, nothing but words, the objects in the room lined up in the order of words, to form those confused and irksome phrases that he who knows how will read. Boredom . . . such awful boredom. . . . How sickening! How very annoying!" This conjugation of words and objects is a metacommentary on the texture of the story. Centered on the barely coherent ramblings of a woman who attempts to wait patiently in her room for the return of her absent husband and children while clearly on the verge of nervous hysteria, the story is recounted largely through a listing of a multitude of objects that decorate her cluttered chambers; these objects define her as she attempts to define herself in them. Objects and words—the "words" of her preverbal ramblings and the words of the text that mirrors them as narrative are disjointed metonymies whose pattern mimics the fragmented nature of her psyche.

The story moves on two interrelated planes. First, we have a sequence of consecutive states or actions: her leisured indolence, her husband's leave-taking (he attempts endearments but she rebuffs him with ill humor), her recollection of a night on the town in the company of her husband and a business associate during which she got drunk but maintained her ladylike bearing, her inventory of things she should be doing before her husband and children return, her vulgar self-disparagement—" 'you slut' "—with which the text closes. Second, we see her consciousness move back and forth between narcissistic self-appreciation (her privileged station, her Portuguese origins, her good taste and sophisticated appearance even when she is seriously inebriated) and the anguished pangs of despair in the face of her aimless existence and all-consuming abulia. The two planes converge in the sense of anomie toward the objects in her bedroom and the outburst of hysterical self-denunciation that closes the text.

Throughout the story the interior monologue underscores not only the woman's vacuous spiritual being, but her inability to provide herself with a coherent self-image. Contrast these two passages, one built around the description of a privileged "poetic" lifestyle, the other focused on barely contained mental dissolution, although even the first positive passage is not free of negative connotations that foreshadow her subsequent hysteria:

Oh what a succulent room! Here she was, fanning herself in Brazil. The sun, trapped in the blinds, shimmered on the wall like the strings of a guitar. Riachuelo Street shook under the gasping weight of the trolley cars which came from Mem de Sá Street. Curious and impatient, she listened to the vibrations of the china cabinet in the drawing room. Impatiently she rolled over to lie face downward, and, sensuously stretching the toes of her dainty feet, she awaited her next thought with opened eyes. "Whosoever found, searched," she said to herself in the form of a rhymed refrain, which always ended up sounding like some maxim. Until eventually she fell asleep with her mouth wide open, her saliva staining the pillow.

She was sitting up in bed, resigned and skeptical. And this was nothing yet. God only knew—she was perfectly aware that this was nothing yet. At this moment things were happening to her that would only hurt later and in earnest. When restored to her normal size, her anesthetized body would start to wake up, throbbing, and she would begin to pay for those big meals and drinks. Then, since this would really end up happening, I might as well open my eyes right now (which she did) and then everything looked smaller and clearer, without her feeling any pain. Everything, deep down, was the same, only smaller and more familiar. She was sitting quite upright in bed, her stomach so full, absorbed and resigned, with the delicacy of one who sits waiting until her partner awakens.

Lispector, as should be evident from these two quotations, is not interested in analysis, psychological or sociologic, of the conflicting emotions or the alternation between trite commonplaces of well-being and compulsive urges of self-destruction. Her characters are unable to engage in any sustained form of introspection and self-analysis (when the protagonist of "Devaneio" sits before her mirror, she sees nothing more than her triply reflected image), and the narrator, as stated, moves between articulating the characters' preverbal stream of consciousness and highlighting metonymic gestures and objects. The result is an atmosphere of oppressive inconsequentiality due to absence of symbols that would suggest significant behavior on the part of the characters. A satisfactory reading of Lispector's stories in *Laços de família* can only be successful if the reader is able to chart the contradictions between the repetitive banalities concerning the fortunate role of women and the inarticulate despair with which her women review their allegedly privileged station in life.

• • •

Another important short-story writer of foreign birth is Samuel Rawet, born in Poland in 1929. His collection, *Contos do imigrante* (1956; Immigrant Stories) is noteworthy. Although these stories may be read for their documentary value as regards the social and psychological experience of the immigrant in "exotic" Brazil, Rawet's elements of surrealism and Borgesian fantasy demand a deeper reading in terms of a basic human violence and intrapersonal tension. Man's experiential reality is seen as a problematic and unstable relationship with unknown forces that threaten to engulf him. The result is an especially disorienting experience for the reader, who is often unable to identify the hidden danger, and it is this vagueness that lends Rawet's stories their particular flavor and suggestive density.

Magical Realism

It would be difficult to overestimate the role of João Guimarães Rosa (1908–1967) in modern Brazilian literature. If Machado de Assis is the giant of nineteenth-century fiction in Brazil, Rosa is clearly the twentieth-century point of reference, particularly as part of the so-called boom of Latin American fiction in the 1960s and inclusion of his works in the many collections translated into English and other languages of the last twenty years.

In a certain sense Rosa is the culmination of the modernist legacy that dominated Brazilian literature for almost fifty years after the Week of Modern Art in São Paulo in 1922. Rosa's writings manifest belief in the privileged position of literary language, which would allow for a transcendence destroyed by modern technology; he similarly proposes the possibility of a cultural syncretism that would revitalize the national character (see the Mexican José Vasconcelos's *La raza Cósmica* [1925; The Cosmic Race]). His language is poetic in the sense that it is highly symbolic and displays neologistic, metaphoric, and metonymic processes that make it difficult to follow for even a native speaker (see in particular his masterful novel *Grande sertao: Veredas* [1956; The Devil to Pay in the Backlands]). Like Juan Rulfo in Mexico, José María Arguedas in Peru, or Gabriel García Márquez in Colombia, Rosa's works synthesize specific Latin American sociocultural concerns and a mythic pattern that demonstrated Latin Americans could write universal novels. This fiction has had considerable international reverberations, in part for its concern for showing the problematic and dialectical relationship between Third-World cultures and the dominant themes of Western society.

The story "As margens da alegria" (1962; "The Thin Edge of Happiness") may be seen as an example of the so-called magical realism Rosa shares with many of the writers of the 1960s. Almost allegorical, the story involves a young boy's innocent interpretation of the impact of modern technology on the jungle when he is taken to visit a new city being carved out of the wilderness. The story dwells on the child's sense of despair as machines and men slash through the intoxicating tropical beauty urban dwellers rarely behold. Told almost in a once-upon-a-time fashion, the story uses a trivial circumstance to suggest a series of oppositions between nature and the machine as perceived intuitively by a child unable to articulate his sudden sense of loss:

More than an anecdote concerning the brutal shattering of youthful and innocent happiness, Rosa's text foregrounds, through the boy's mediating consciousness, a paradigmatic Latin American conflict: the natural vs. the mechanical, spontaneous sentiment vs. artificial power—in a word, what is human vs. what is artificial and therefore destructive. Where U.S. society might typically see the union of the mechanical and the human toward the greater comfort of the latter, a text like Rosa's sees the two as irremediably antagonistic: the boy's loss of innocence is not the product of any routine process of maturation, whereby the child comes to harmonious terms with modern mechanized society. Rather it is the result of the brutal imposition of the new mechanized society (the adult representatives of progress and their machines, for whom the beauties of nature discovered by the boy are at best food and at worst a nuisance) on an awesome nature. It is only when the boy's perception of his new surroundings have been "conditioned" by the attitudes and action of the adults that he sees the new reality as no longer a fairyland but as a threatening and dark void: "The boy could not understand it. The forest, the black trees, were much too much, they were the world."[3]

"A terceira margem do rio" ("The Third Bank of the River") from *Primeiras estórias* (1962; *The Third Bank of the River*) may be read on one level as a superb example of Rosa's concern for the interplay between conventions of society and deep-seated atavistic urges in the human spirit that shatter those conventions when they can no longer be contained. Such topics have long been treated by the grotesque, the horror story, and the war anti-epic, where the features of human nature glossed over by polite society break through the ordered surface in particularly gruesome (and often tiresomely stereotyped) fashion. In a writer of Rosa's subtlety, the incursion of hidden urges appears as a pattern of behavior that departs from the accepted code. Moreover, disruption of the conventional scheme is described by confusion and bewilderment at something that has transcended anything that can be accounted for rationally.

"Terceira margem" is, if one may be permitted the oxymoron, an understated hyperbolic parable of one individual's abandonment of conventional social responsibility. The narrator's father decides one day to make a canoe for himself; over the protestations of his wife and ignoring the consternation of his children, he sets himself adrift in the canoe, never to return to shore again. Against the backdrop of his periodic reappearances in the middle of the river, the life of the family follows its conventional course: the children grow up, his wife decides to move in with her sister, yet the father sits impassive in his canoe in midstream, oblivious of the human society he has abandoned. "Our father never came back. He hadn't gone anywhere. He stuck to that stretch of the river, staying halfway across, always in the canoe, never to spring out of it, ever again. The strangeness of that truth was enough to dismay us all. What had never been before, was. Our relatives, the neighbors, and all our acquaintances met and took counsel together."

The key to the effectiveness of Rosa's story is the framing of "the strangeness of that truth." Were the story to refer to the impact on a family of a father who simply picks up and disappears, it would be no more than the fictional narrative of a sociologic phenomenon common not only in Brazil but in all societies, where providers disappear either because of economic pressures or unwillingness to be confined by conventional homelife. Indeed, one reasonable interpretation of the text is in terms of the baleful effects of a still-prevailing remoteness of fathers in Brazilian society. Rosa's story is, however, "strange" because the father haunts his abandoned family with his periodic reappearances in the middle of the river. He has become a phantom figure who returns neither to resume his former role nor to disrupt the new routine of his home, but only to drift impassively by, tormenting them with his physical and spiritual distance. "He never felt the need to know anything about us; had he no family affection?" It is the inexplicableness, not of the father's decision to abandon his family, but the unique and startling form his separation takes that makes the narrative so disconcerting and ambiguous.

"Terceira margem" is narrated by one of the sons who grows from boyhood to manhood in the lapse between his father's departure and the telling of the story. As narrator he conveys all of the bewilderment of his family and society at large in the face of such a singular action. Although he speaks in a matter-of-fact tone about the events leading to his father's departure and about subsequent developments, he is as much at a loss to interpret them as everybody else is: "We just had to try to get used to it. But it was hard, and we never really managed. I'm judging by myself, of course. Whether I wanted to or not, my thoughts kept circling back and I found myself thinking of father."

Thus the narrative is a surplus of statements concerning what happened and how people reacted to it, but a paucity of interpretation as to why the father took such an unusual step, why he chose to haunt his family rather than just disappear for good, and why no one could adjust to what could be dismissed as the man's weird but inconsequential eccentricity. The narrator's own confusion and the anguish of abandonment that he conveys result in an aura of uncertain meaning. That the event had such a profound impact on the family and neighbors and so clearly haunts the memory of the narrator to become an all-consuming obsession invites the reader to share in the desire for a rational explanation, which is not forthcoming.

The narrator obliquely (unconsciously?) indicates that there is a much greater symbolic meaning in the story than that of domestic crisis brought about by curious eccentricity. The singularity of the event and the narrator's inability to provide an interpretation that would reduce it to manageable proportions leads inevitably to reading "Terceira margem" as an existential parable on man's abandonment by God. Not only is the father described in hierarchical terms that establish the characters as a duplication of a patriarchal theology in microcosm, but throughout the narration, events mimic a liturgy of veneration and propitiation. Thus when the daughter's child is born, she presents him to the father in an act of baptismal offering:

When my sister had a baby boy, she got it into her head that she must show father his grandson. All of us went and stood on the bluff. The day was fine and my sister was wearing the white dress she had worn at her wedding. She lifted the baby up in her arms and her husband held a parasol over the two of them. We called and we waited. Our father didn't come. My sister wept; we all cried and hugged one another as we stood there.

As the other family members, out of disgust and despair, fall away and desist in their hope that the man will return, only the narrator remains, committed to waiting for a father who will neither return nor explain himself. Therefore when at the end of the text, the narrator, obsessed with his lonely vigil at the edge of the river, believes his father has responded to his attempts at communication, we do not know if God has relented in his self-imposed isolation from his son, or if it is only the wish-fulfilling hallucination of the faithful but crazed votiary: "For he seemed to be coming from the hereafter. And I am pleading, pleading, pleading for forgiveness."

Significantly, Rosa's story is not written as an allegory, and description is limited to concrete—even trivial—details of domestic life in the Brazilian backlands. But the strangeness of the father's unexplained decision and the controlling reference of the title to an illogical "third bank of the river" result in ambiguity that translates the story of one man's flight from conventional domestic responsibility into a parable of existential despair over God's abandonment of his children and the loss of the integrated human society promised by the theologies of divine presence.

$$\bullet \quad \bullet \quad \bullet$$

Nélida Piñon (1937–   ) is representative of a very active group of women writers in Brazil who have followed Clarice Lispector in receiving the same level of recognition as the men who continue to dominate the country's culture (the Brazilian Academy of Letters currently has no

women members). Names such as Raquel de Queiroz (1910–   ),
Leila Assunçao (1944?–   ) Ruth Bueno (?–   ), Lygia Fagundes
Telles (1923–   ), and Dinah Silveira de Queiroz (1910–   ), who
was the first woman to receive the prestigious Machado de Assis prize
awarded by the Brazilian Academy, join that of Piñon as women writers
of an international stature. None of these authors can in any strict sense
be called feminist writers (as Lispector can, although she was not
preoccupied exclusively with women's issues). Rather, their works are
more concerned with the role of the individual in society, although
perhaps affecting women more because of the traditional strictures
placed on their range of activities. Piñon in particular focuses on the
confrontation between her characters and the social codes or value
systems that circumscribe what is appropriate behavior and what constitutes conduct that will be classified by convention as deviant, lunatic,
or suspect. This confrontation is often handled with a mordant humor
that underscores the bewilderment of men and women in society and
their frustrated attempts to come to terms with a structure that seems
more to trap and humiliate them than to give them a significant place in
the community.

The title story of Piñon's 1973 collection, *Sala de armas* (Trophy
Room), bears a remarkable similarity to Rosa's "Terceira margem,"
although her story is told in the first person. A man decides to separate
himself from life, to construct a room in which he will die, surrounded
by the treasures accumulated by his apparent avarice. Regardless of the
anger of his wife and the distress of his sons, whom he hopes will follow
his example, he made a choice early in life, then lived in abulic fashion
staring at the cathedral like ceiling he has constructed with the
emblems, the heraldic symbols, of his life, waiting patiently through the
years for his death. The story is essentially an allegory of the tight
network of social conventions that bind us to belief in an illusion of life
as the normal state, and the relations of human intercourse as a permanent set of ties that binds us forever. When an individual chooses
deliberately to flout this set of beliefs and to flaunt his preparation for
man's inevitable "journey" in death, the result is havoc in his immediate
community, as though recognition of the inevitable were, in fact, radical deviance (abulia, of course is classified as a mental illness, as are
many of the forms of obsession that the narrator describes).

There is yet another superficial coincidence with Rosa's story: the
narrator speaks of his "passion," of his "right to live in accord with his
own stigmata," of how people "probably ask themselves: Who among

us should put himself on the cross, nailing his hands and feet with diamond spikes and making himself the universal heir" (the phrase in Portuguese, *herdeiro universal*, also means residuary legatee, a synonymy that enhances the coincidences in the story between the narrator's Christologic self-assessment and the legal conventions of his arrangements for the proper disposition of his property on his death). His wife refuses ever to vist him in his shrine, in the trophy room where, as a knight of his own destiny, he keeps his chosen solitary vigil. He is visited by his sons, however, who bring him prayers and offerings as though, in a parody of obvious theological and patriarchal motifs, they were enacting an intensely religious ritual.

There are symbolic dimensions to Piñon's text and the narrator's self-apotheosis in an attempt to justify his lonely decision to separate himself from the so-called normal community of mankind. (In an accommodation of the motif of "Father forgive them, for they know not what they do," he says of his wife "She believed in the immortality of life, and I, more sinister, invented the immortality of death and prepared myself for the banquet.") This symbology is reinforced by the description of his father's self-wrought separation from mankind. His father retreated into the woods, where he laboriously dug a pit that would serve as a grave not only for himself but for all of his personal effects— his bed, his hunting gear, his seeds for planting, his dog, his horse, his everyday clothes. "He planned the banquet and celebrated it alone. . . . Then he died. . . . I was the only one to lament his loss." Thus the narrator establishes a father-son continuity (enhanced by his desire that his own eldest son follow him in sacrificial ritual) that unquestionably reverberates with Christian allusions. In this sense, the text establishes a relationship that transcends the opposition between a psychotic and a bewildered society, and juxtaposes a putatively mystic ritual (although it must be remembered that the narrator engages in his own careful self-characterization) and a social community that willfully ignores the true end of life.

Is Piñon's story serious in its treatment of a profound existential commitment on the part of its protagonist-narrator, or does it lampoon the narrator's self-serving identification with a religious passion? One of the curious features of "Sala de armas" is that the text mediates between circumstance and the individual. Locked in a holy mutism that allows him to communicate with his "vestal" sons only through eye movements, the narrator communicates verbally by means of the text with the reader who is not a member of his immediate social nucleus.

On the verge of death ("But, despite my intense passion, death seems not to want me. There are still a few hours, a few days left, I know. Ah, how difficult it is to wait."), the narrator is nevertheless permitted to tell his own story in detail to the disembodied reader. The latter is then left to judge as best as possible whether or not that narrative possesses coherence as the sincere *vita* of a modern saint whose intense self-characterization is a correlate of his religious passion. The lack of verisimilitude in this narration, as opposed to the more conventional form of a diary maintained by the saint in his or her lonely vigil, lends an unquestionably ironic tone to Piñon's story.

It is difficult to determine if the narrator of "Sala de armas" has structured a detailed and internally coherent explanation of the reasons for his holy sacrifice, or if that explanation represents nothing more than the delusions of a psychotic grasping at a confused set of grandiose religious symbols in an attempt to justify his failure to commit himself to the tedious demands of social intercourse. In the first case, his sons' reverence is understandable; in the second, his wife's angry repudiation of his behavior is only to be expected. The literary interest of Piñon's text springs precisely from vagueness over this crucial issue, and we are left with only the self-contemplation of an individual who, in either case, is a cripple in terms of the demands of a healthy, well-adjusted society:

> I know that my wife will not accompany me on the funeral pyre. Just as she promised, she has never returned to the room. She has never spoken my name, never asked about my health, about how many scabs have appeared on this body after so many years. Perhaps she exultantly imagines me dead. However this hope will not comfort her for long. We are watchful of each other as though we were seeing each other, and in some obscure way we still stimulate each other. I have grown used to her footsteps conquering the hall constructed inside the room so that she could get to the kitchen and other rooms without seeing me. This fury has ended up branding my soul.

One of the topics of contemporary literature is the way in which discourse is a method by which the individual attempts to find meaning in experience that may have no independent verification or validity, but that is a powerful personal myth because it has resulted from his or her own creative efforts. Julio Cortázar's (1914–   ) Horacio Oliveira is responsible for one of the most profound bogus myths of the contemporary Latin American novel in *Rayuela* (1963; *Hopscotch*), that of a Paris-based Latin American pseudoexistential. Augusto Roa Basto's (1918–   ) *Yo el Supremo* (1974; *I the Supreme*) is the monologue of

Latin America's first great dictator, Francia of Paraguay, who attempts through a series of ambiguous, contradictory, and self-annihilating discourses to justify his benevolent tyranny.

The Microtext

One of the most important forms of contemporary Brazilian narrative is the microtext. Although it does not have any special name in Portuguese, it appears in the work of a number of important writers and echoes similar variants of the short story: in Argentina, Jorge Luis Borges in *El hacedor* (1960; *Dreamtigers*), Julio Cortázar *Historias de cronopios y famas* (1962; *Cronopios and Famas*), and Marco Denevi in *Falsificaciones* (1966; *Falsifications*); in Mexico, Juan José Arreola in *Confabulario* (1952; *Confabulario*); in Cuba, Guillermo Cabrera Infante in *Vista del amanecer en el trópico* (1975; *View of Dawn in the Tropics*); and in the United States, Donald Barthelme.

The microtext is not to be confused with equally brief examples of the *crónica*: the chronicle is an essay or journalistic form that may encapsulate personal commentary in a mini-narrative to illustrate a point. Writers such as Art Buchwald often make an exaggeratedly ironic point by means of such a mini-narrative, one whose ad hoc fictionality is obvious. The microtext is exclusively a narrative statement, without pragmatic commentary. It may run from a few lines to a maximum of one or two pages, and the "event" described may be so schematic that the text simply reminds one of the tradition of biblical parables, although again the parable usually relies on a particular point to carry it. The parable tradition was continued in the Middle Ages, often in secular modes, by the exemplum. To whatever extent the exempla are detachable from their larger context, they are forerunners of the microtext, as are the Italian *novelline* ("novelettes") and the long-standing practice of producing humor in the form of a comic narrative—for example, a shaggy-dog story.

The point is that the microtext may possess a certain status as a sub-genre because of its apparent refutation of the conventions of the modern short story, especially with reference to the development of an attitude toward a specific event. In reality, however, it has its roots in forms that antedate the classic modern short story as exemplified by Poe and the like, and are considered its primitive precursors. To understand the role played by the microtext at least in contemporary Brazilian and Spanish American literature, emphasis must be placed on its relation to

supposedly primitive forms of storytelling. Like these forms, the microtext lacks emphasis on detailed creation of mood and on the singular
event narrated to show the underlying logic of its occurrence and its
consequences for the individuals touched by it. The microtext does not
strive for a highly concentrated synedoche of human existence; it is
more metonymic: the discourse, which may not be precisely narrative,
refers, often elliptically, to a set of phenomena the greatest importance
of which lies in having been chosen for inclusion in a literary discourse.
Although the microtext may describe a situation or tell a parablelike
story, the significance of what is grouped together depends on the
reader's need to discover symbolic meaning.

For example, in the collection by Dalton Trevisan (1925–   ), "Os
mistérios de Curitiba" (The Mysteries of Curitiba) and in *Desastres do
amor* (1968; Disasters of Love), a series of microtexts focuses on aspects
of life in a modern city. The author's apparent concern is to demonstrate
how individuals are separated from the poetry of life and from their
inherent humanity by the dehumanization of the industrial and commercial metropolis. Significantly, the title word "mysteries" stresses the
desire to probe the unknown. Here, the circumstances described are
mysterious both in the sense of a circumstance that resists our understanding of it and in the generic sense of exemplary and dramatic
spectacles portraying biblical events. Trevisans's stories are mysteries in
their concentration on a circumstance that may superficially appear to
be insignificant, and also because they draw their material from the
spectacle of modern urban life and suggest transcendent meaning behind its apparently trivial details.

In "Bonde" (Train), a tired businessman, restlessly trying to relieve the
discomfort of a callus on his foot by shifting his posture, awaits the train
to work. He fantasizes as to what he coud be doing in the half-hour of
routine travel on the train: "João could have done great things in that
half hour of life stolen by the train: drink rum from Jamaica, kiss
Mercedes, sack an island." These possibilities lead him to elaborate a
vision of himself as a pirate captain. The train is his ship on the high seas,
and speculation as to his bounty becomes entwined with his real-life
commercial activities. In this way, the boredom of a routine life and the
aches of a middle-aged body are set aside by a rich (if cliche-ridden)
fantasy that replaces meaningless reality with a poetic vision of romantic lawlessness.

The story parallels the details of conventional life, as exemplified by
the unenthusiastic businessman, with those of pirate life: the train is the

ship, his fellow passengers are crew members, their clothes transformed into pirate garb. Two specific details underscore the extravagant transformations of meaning the character has devised. A young man who asks where the train goes, receives the swashbuckling reply, "For a million stinking vermin." When an elderly man carrying a bundle of bananas trips and spills his cargo, the businessman, who has imaginatively turned him into a grizzled buccaneer, picks them up in a gesture of urbane courtesy. Nothing has happened, no real mystery has been either described or probed. The entire text deals summarily with a trivial set of circumstances, the unimaginative fantasy of a tired commuter.

One of Trevisan's most effective microtexts, with its disturbing conjunction of the grotesque and commonplaces of landscape poetry, is the title story of the collection *Cemitério de elefantes* (1964, The Elephants' Graveyard). the story is told by a matter-of-fact narrator who relates in elliptic tropes the fact that his city includes a "cemetery for drunks." This cemetery is like a wild animal habitat or preserve, and the individuals who populate it are venerated by the townspeople. The area, a combination mangrove swamp and tropical skid row, appears when measured against the sociocultural code of a Western reader, to be nothing more or less than a slum district inhabited by socially marginal characters like drunks, lepers, and other pariahs. Yet the narrator speaks as though his audience could accept the assertion that there exists a park of veritable holy men revered by the citizens who take them offerings of fish and speak to them from a distance as though addressing virtuous monks. The details provided by the narrator are nevertheless unequivocable: the cemetery is a realm of untouchables who are dying of what appears to be leprosy or elephantiasis and who, as their flesh putrifies, subsist by fighting with each other for the mango roots, the ingá fruit, and the fish provided by the townspeople.

The landscape poetry suggests a realm between a moonlit renaissance garden of monsters and the *locus amoenus* of a holy Garden of Eden: the references to the tropical plants, the marble decorations, the moonwashed inhabitants. But this is inverted by the application of specific details of this cemetery of rotting human flesh. Thus the elephants are not the noble beasts of some jungle park, but human beings ravaged by a leprous disease, the marble decorations are in fact the broken bottles with which the drunks litter the ground, and the lyric moonlight washes the swollen members of the dying: "Chico disappears into the sacred graveyard among the skeletons of grotesque feet that rise up in the moonlight."

"Cemetério" is an excellent example of microtext in that there is no narrative to speak of, but rather, descriptive evocation. In this case, the literary interest of that evocation does not lie with the mimetic accuracy of well-chosen descriptive language. Instead, the artistic density derives from the contradiction of a swamp of drunken and diseased human beings presented as a preserve of venerated holy men. The implied oxymoron of a cemetery of living dead is developed through interplay between lyricism and the grotesqueness of a certain variety of human fate.

Dalton Trevisan is perhaps the most successful writer of narrative microtexts in contemporary Brazilian literature, but an anthology of this genre would include many other names, such as Clarice Lispector, Rubem Braga, and Rubem Fonseca.

Neoexpressionalist Forms of Social Protest

Major political upheavals in Latin America inevitably have had an impact on cultural and literary development. Because of the refocusing of national goals and values they imply and, never to be underestimated, the draconian restrictions they impose on artistic expression during at least an initial phase of upheaval, such events can only be avoided by the most unshakable neutral writer or artist. In 1973 in Chile and Uruguay, 1976 in Argentina (and, projecting long forward shadows, 1930 and 1946), 1959 in Cuba, and 1964 in Brazil new stages of respective national cultures were ushered in. Brazilian society has only begun, since the late 1970s, to emerge from the 1964 coup with a considerable relaxation of direct censorship and political oppression. Thus ends a phase of chaotic sociopolitical life that was paralleled by a period of intense cultural accomplishments.

The harsh realities of the military dictatorship and renewed economic inequities brought about by the much-touted Brazilian economic miracle of the late 1960s and early 1970s resulted in a group of writers whose artistic vision was unflinchingly fixed on the ugliest aspects of national life. One can say that with these writers, Brazilian literature had definitively put aside the ideals of the vanguard modernist movement of the 1920s. Like European modernism, the Brazilian movement stressed the redeeming features of art, and its version of neoprimitivism was to extol its indigenous element and examine the possibility of constructing a synthetic national culture by blending the jungle and the city. The ravages of internal migration toward the cities, the destruction of Indian groups with construction of the Trans-Amazonian highway and the incursion of foreign capitalism in the backlands, and the restoration of government by and for a technocratic oligarchy, all combined to undermine the romantic myths of Brazilian culture and to foment despair over the virtually insoluble social problems that Brazil shared with Latin America and the Third World as a whole.

A writer such as Rubem Fonseca (1925–   ) whose first books antedate the 1964 revolution, but whose importance belongs to the postdemocratic period, shares with a broad spectrum of Latin American writers the imperative to discredit complacent cultural myths and social bromides. These writers seek to underscore the destructive violence of a society in which human values have no serious structural or institutional reality, and in which senseless killings, degrading eroticism, and brutal social intercourse are commonplace, systematic inversions of Christian ethics. One critic has referred to Rubem Fonseca's work as indicative of the "underground story," an appellation that is appropriate to the extent that literature of this sort has had a precarious existence all over Latin America. Denounced alternately as immoral and pornographic or as politically seditious and socially destructive, such negative literature often has international distribution because the authors cannot publish in their own countries. (The case of the Argentine Manuel Puig is particularly instructive in this regard.)

Of special significance to postmodernist writers like Fonseca, is the image of language. One may profitably contrast Fonseca with João Guimarães Rosa, the best example in contemporary literature of a continuation of the modernist concept of poetic language that mediates between worn superficial reality and deeper ("third bank of the river") meanings. For writers like Fonseca, though, the gritty and jarring qualities of colloquial language are more a natural poetry to be recovered, *Black Orpheus* style, by the artist, than they are metonyms of the social degradation of those who utter them. The street language of José Agustín and Gustavo Sainz in Mexico, Manuel Puig and Enrique Medina in Argentina, and Pedro Juan Soto and Emilio Díaz Valcárcel in Puerto Rico seek to show how disruptive speech is an antiesthetically eloquent correlate of man's social fall. Such a belief constitutes a serious challenge to the cultural concepts of language and other artistic media as ennobling forces. If socially revolutionary writers like Miguel Angel Asturias (Guatemala) and Pablo Neruda (Chile) believed in a poetic language, postmodernist authors such as Fonseca clearly subscribe to a concept of literature as anti-art in a way that bespeaks a despairing perception of an irremediably fragmented society.

Fonseca's "O exterminador" (1969, The Exterminator) is a sort of pseudoscience fiction tale concerning a terrorist operation to exterminate a Governor General set at some undefined future time. It is written in ten relatively brief sections in a matter-of-fact manner that imparts the tone of a bureaucratic report. The story describes the initiation of the terrorist plan and the Governor General's attempt to abort that plan, the terrorist-inspired street-rioting in the ghettos of Copacabana and Ipanema, the torture of one of the terrorist leaders, and the final assassination of the Governor General by an exterminator, the very man he appointed to head the counterterrorist operation.

Fonseca's text is science fiction in its time setting, in the series of futuristic modifications of details known to the informed contemporary reader (e.g., the fact that the two present-day elegant residential areas, Copacabana and Ipanema, have become miserable slums), in the abundance of advanced technological concepts ("PERSAB, 'the abbreviation for Absolute Persuasion,' an instrument of physical torture. Not to be confused with PERCOM, abbreviation for Compulsive Persuasion, also an instrument of torture, but only psychic in nature"), and in the congestion of acronyms and their parenthetical clarification. The story is ironic and leans toward parody, hence the qualification pseudoscience fiction. For example, the semantics are a projection into the future contemporary sociopolitical ills of Latin American republics like Brazil, where social and economic conditions have created an endless circle of unrest, terrorism, governmental oppression, further public distrust of institutions, and similar upheavals. As the avuncular torturer says to his young apprentice: "This is an easy job to do. Let me give you some advice: grab this opportunity by tooth and nail. You'll have a good job here for the rest of your life. As long as the nature of our people stays the same, you've got it made. And it would be impossible to change the nature of our people, don't you think?" Also ironic is the reference to the different regional accents of the exterminators, who may be members of an elite, highly trained, and sophisticated terrorist organization but who still, in this futuristic society, have the distinctive regional accents that classify people socioculturally in contemporary Brazil.

One section of the story appears to be completely superfluous and its presence seems to confirm the author's tongue-in-cheek rewriting of modern events. Section 3 concerns the exterminator's visit to a hotel for sexual assignations. At the entrance is the cautionary announcement: "If you haven't known the man/woman with you for a long time, don't go to bed with him/her. Protect your life." The description of the erotic encounter between the exterminator and the prostitute (who remarks, in another oblique reference to modern Brazilian culture, "If the people really paid attention to that advice, no one would ever go to bed with anyone else again.") is a combination of sadomasochistic fantasy and the opportunity for yet another list of technical references and acronyms.

The fact that the author spends a considerable amount of time providing italicized parenthetical clarifications of the acronyms provides a curious and contradictory texture to the story. On the one hand, the reader will grasp very quickly that this is a parable on continuation into the future of senseless violence that springs from oppressive injustices of Brazilian society. In this sense, the story is serious because both the nature of that violence and its seeming permanence are dreadful facts of life (Fonseca's story was published at a time when official violence was particularly acute in Brazil). On the other hand, the need to dress up the story with futuristic references indicates the need to clarify such details, with the result that the parenthetical commentaries become devices to slow down the orderly exposition of the plot.

Such a pattern of retardation is, of course, not a defect of Fonseca's story, but a major factor in his handling of the cliches of the predictable set of relationships. Indeed, the text does not, in its elaboration of events, rise above the hackneyed level of a television serial. This lack of originality, where the only surprise is the fact that the security agent is also the exterminator, and the slackening of tempo by the parenthetical comments and other extraneous elements, is part of Fonseca's conscious artistic choice. His story is a spoof of a certain type of James Bond science fiction, and its disruptive features are ironic references to that form of popular culture. Satirizing second-rate literature leads even to a few examples of outright silliness, as when the narrator defines, because it is presumably new gadgetry, what the modern reader is familiar with:

> "This is the routine: when the operation is done, CONTROL is consulted and it decides, in accord with an electronic computer, where the prisoner is to be sent, if he is to be liquidated or recovered," explained the old guard. (*CONTROL: Control.*)
> The guard turned the INTERCOM on and asked for CONTROL.
> (*INTERCOM: Direct intercommunication.*)

The foregoing does not mean that Fonseca's story is itself inferior. Rather, the references to a very real sociopolitical problem in Brazil underlines the burlesquing of a particular mode of popular, escapist literature. The challenge to the reader lies in the need to grasp this central meaning that lies beyond the exterior trappings of hackneyed adventure or science fiction, as well as the irony and various devices for slowing the narrative flow that give the story the appearance of spoof. In turn, Fonseca's handling of the material, where there is a deliberately uneasy balance of social commentary, satire of popular culture, and humorous accommodation of tropes, demonstrate the break with "good" literature that he strives for in his debasement of both high and popular culture.

Even more original in his creative use of pop material is Roberto Drummond (1940–   ); see his *A morte de D.J. em Paris* (1975, The Death of D. J. in Paris).

Although all major Latin American literature can claim writers who are either in the mainstream of Western science fiction or whose expressionistic fantasies are at least close cousins, Brazil has an unusually large number of highly skilled practioners such as André Carneiro (1922–   ) and José J. Veiga (1915–   ). In Veiga's fiction, strange phenomena become correlates of man's existential sense of a constant and imminent threat to the stability and continuity of his world. Reality as a fixed point of reference circumscribed by an individual's self-satisfied perception is challenged by characters who are unable to cope with the invasion—often physically violent, always psychologically threatening—of the inexplicable.

The opening sentence of the title story of the 1968 collection *A máquina extraviada* (The Misplaced Machine) is indicative of Veiga's handling of this material: "You are always asking for news about things here in the backlands, and finally I can tell you about something important." This introit, spoken as though beginning a gossipy letter, goes on to describe an "imposing machine which is making everybody all excited." In the fifteen paragraphs of this short work, the narrator makes the transition from commenting on the chance arrival in the backwater of the latest example of industrial technology, to the sense of wonder at the presence of an object that has no apparent function and that no one knows how to operate. Thus the imposing piece of hardware, passive and inert, restructures by its mere presence the attitudes of the townspeople who are caught up in the intense activity of attempting to ascertain its origin, function, and purpose. This concern becomes so all-engrossing that the machine assumes a mystical quality, and a miracle has already been attributed to it.

Veiga closes his text by a very effective inversion of technological and scientific explanation. The narrator dreads the day when some technician will arrive "from the outside" and set the machine to doing whatever it was meant to do. If this happens, all of the magic of the object will be lost, and the explanation of its function will represent a loss of identity for the rural townspeople who have redefined themselves in terms of the talisman. Behind the narrator's sense of wonder lies a truly humorous statement concerning technological progress in the Third World.

If Fonseca handles the flotsam and jetsam of contemporary Brazilian society through the comic parody of popular culture, writers such as Luíz Fernando Emediato (1951–   ) manifest all of the pent-up rage of a generation of artists blocked from giving free rein to the dissection of their society. Emediato has emerged as one of the most forceful writers of the post-1964 generation in Brazil. Indeed, for many he must seem the most strident as well as the most distasteful, or even tasteless. His literature is unquestionably explicit in ways designed to attract all kinds of attention: from the government's opposition forces as a vocal spokesman for their frustrating and continually frustrated cause; and from the government's powerful supporters as precisely the sort of writer Brazil can very well do without. His writings exemplify whatever thaw one may legitimately speak of in the difficult situation for literature and the arts in that country since 1964.

A rebeliao dos mortos (1978; The Rebellion of the Dead) is a carefully organized collection of short stories unified by variations on the issue of cultural, spiritual, and political violence in Brazil. The divisions of the collection are signposts for the key manifestations of oppression, and the general sense of frustration is symbolized by the image of the Brazilian citizenry as varieties of the walking dead, zombies for whom there is no escape, no transcendence, no stimulus for life in any of the positive senses adduced by Western civilization. Book I, *Patriotismo* (Patriotism); consists of a long Dos Passos-like "A data magna do nosso calendário Cívico" (The greatest date on our civic calendar), a series of vignettes that weave together various forms of death for exemplary citizens on Brazil's principal national holiday. Book II, *Sexo* (Sex) is made up of four works that see sex, particularly in cultural and political biases concerning its role in human endeavors, as a powerful agent of oppression. *Vegetal* (Vegetal) is particularly noteworthy as a continuation of Lispector's writings on the sterility of the lot of middle-class women and as a startling frank presentation of female erotic fantasies. Book III is the heart of the collection: *Fantasía (mais nem tanto)* (Fantasy [but not too much]), consists of the one story, "Anatomia do pesadelo" [Anatomy of the nightmare], which is an allegory in very inventive terms of the "Castle" of the Brazilian police state. In Book IV, *Violência* (Violence), the first "Um estranho à porta" (A Stranger at the Door), is a noteworthy Brazilian adaptation of Kafka's *Trial* in its exhaustive detail describing the caprices of the limitless power of the representatives of so-called public order in a police state. Finally, the closing text, the title story, is a kind of pseudodocumentary based on a symbolic rebellion of the "dead" against their plight.

Emediato's literature is frankly contentious. The closest parallel is to be found in Augusto Roa Bastos's stories concerning political oppression—and consequently spiritual deprivation—in Paraguay, *El trueno entre las hojas* (1955; Thunder Among the Leaves). One could also refer to the calculated fury of Cabrera Infante's "history" of hundreds of years of political oppression in Cuba, *Vista del amanecer en el trópico* (1975; View of Dawn in the Tropics) or his earlier *Así en la paz como en la guerra* (1968; In War as in Peace). Like these, Emediato's collection seems intent on extending literary structures. The perspective is essentially that of a denunciatory omniscient narrator; yet it exploits the virtues of merging the reader's subconscious with the action. This is particularly evident in "Anatomia" (Anatomy) and in "Estranho" (Stranger). The use of kafkaesque expressionist symbols like the individual as a residence whose integrity is violated by the secret police, or the individual as a sexual object sodomized by oppressive authority (the latter a metaphor put to varied use by a writer such as William S. Burroughs) results in stories that are especially startling for their emphatic rhetoric.

Emediato's stories reveal an opportunistic seizing of the right moment to say in print things that had hitherto been inhibited by censorship and political violence in Brazil. This is underscored by the obvious meanings of the stories with a concomitant reduction in expressive density. Yet Emediato is unquestionably indicative of a recent trend in Brazilian brief fiction, one that underlines the precarious and ambiguous social role of the writer in Latin America.

Edilberto Coutinho's (1933–   ) collection, *Maracanã adeus* (1980; Good-Bye, Maracanã), won the 1980 prize for short fiction awarded by Havana's important Casa de las Américas. The fact that it also won an award from the Brazilian Academy of Letters for fiction is quite symbolic of the country's increasingly open attitude toward opposition literature.

Maracanã is a clever and original approach to Brazilian social reality and the worst aspects of commercial, mass popular culture through the device of capitalizing on the paradigmatic role of soccer mania in the lives of vast numbers of Latin Americans. (Perhaps one of the stimuli for Coutinho's stories was Brazil's reaching the final match of the 1978 World Soccer Cup only to lose to host Argentina; the fever pitch in both countries was almost unbearable.)

The stories provide the opportunity for extensive sociolcultural commentary as to how elements of popular culture both define the lifestyle of the masses in a capitalist or protocapitalist society and how such elements may shape the entire value structure of those masses: popular culture is, in this version, a mechanism for social control. Maracanã is the enormous sports stadium in downtown Rio, and it literally looms as a sort of cathedral of soccer in Brazil. Coutinho is essentially a neorealist who is able to zero in on the sterile and untranscendent lives of individuals whose only spiritual peaks, whose only true aspirations are defined by their identification with soccer: the teams, players, managers, matches, betting pools, rivalries, and the complex ways in which the grinding, empty, daily routine in a system from which there is little chance of escape are integrated with the elaborate "fiction" of the sport.

Coutinho's stories implicitly describe the sterile lower-middle-class existence in explicit terms of the sport. Thus their intent is as much literary and sport spectacle as it is sociocultural documentary. Through the use of many stock elements of contemporary narrative, Coutinho leavens the sociologic and gives his stories density of expression that effectively caricatures the reigning sports culture in Brazil.

Conclusion

The brief mention of Emediato's and Coutinho's fiction leads to a new threshold for the Brazilian short story in the 1980s. Although the quality of Brazilian literary production has never seriously waned since the time of Machado de Assis, the country's abiding social and political problems, which reached their worst point in the 1960s, have threatened to silence many of the vigorous and angry young voices. The present conditions nevertheless augur well for the end of the twentieth century, a circumstance one wishes were also true of other countries with major literatures such as Argentina or Chile.

Although this chapter focuses on only a few major writers—and a more extensive treatment would find room for the truly original work of Osman Lins, Autran Dourado, Lygia Fagundes Telles, and many others—it is clear that if Brazilian literature is unquestionably the equal of any Western artistic production, the short story is assuredly one of its strongest components.[4]

David William Foster

Arizona State University, Tempe

THE SPANISH AMERICAN SHORT STORY FROM ECHEVERRIA TO QUIROGA

Naomi Lindstrom

Early History

Spanish American writing may be said to begin with the letters of Christopher Columbus; yet the first piece that can be considered a short story is Esteban Echeverría's 1838(?) "El matadero" (The Slaughtering Grounds). Looking at the year in which the Argentine author is believed to have composed this famous work, one may well wonder how Latin American literature could have developed for over three centuries without producing any brief narrative fiction suitable for consideration in an overview of the continent's short story.

The most obvious of possible answers to this question is that Latin American intellectuals, however talented with words, found relatively little occasion to cultivate such an artistic form. The hectic succession of real-world dilemmas facing educated individuals impelled them toward more pragmatic forms of writing, documents intended to communicate meaning in an immediately useful way. The earliest writings to reflect the Hispanic influx into the New World, generally known as chronicles, are nonfiction descriptive and narrative works. Readers may certainly doubt the objective veracity of these reports, inevitably written by interested parties, but the works of Columbus, Cortés, Bernal Díaz del Castillo, Father Bartolomé de las Casas, and others present themselves as historical representations of fact.

As the colonial society became established, a more reflective approach to writing was possible. In the area of prose, however, the essay

35

still supplanted imaginative work. Close, perhaps, to the fictional narrative are those miscellaneous works rich in anecdotal material. *El lazarillo de los ciegos caminantes entre Buenos Aires y Lima* (1773; *El Lazarillo: A Guide of Inexperienced Travelers between Buenos Aires and Lima,* 1965), sets forth the pseudonymous Concolorcorvo's lively anecdotes of the New World inhabitants' insistence in thinking of themselves as Europeans. Juan Rodríguez Freile's *El carnero* (1636; *The Ram*), abounds with scabrous episodes taken from local oral tradition, yet the work is offered as a historical essay. Beyond any doubt, writers like Concolorcorvo and Freile displayed considerable sophistication in the construction of their narratives. While it might be profitable to study their work for narrative structure, it would be stretching a point to call the anecdotal portions of their writings short stories.

The year 1816 is a landmark in the development of Latin American prose fiction. *El periquillo sarniento* (1816; *The Itching Parrot*), by the Mexican Jose Joaquín Fernández de Lizardi, is indisputably a fully elaborated inventive fiction. Only its length, that of a complete novel, disqualifies it from consideration here. It should certainly be noted, though, that Lizardi did not turn to fiction out of a desire to move away from directly useful writing into a more privileged sphere of art. A conservative turn in the political climate, including reactivation of the Inquisition, forced him to seek more covert strategies for disseminating his enlightenment-influenced views. Lizardi's switch from pamphleteering to narrative is emblematic of the still prevalent use of fiction to publish sociopolitical statements with a minimal degree of risk to the author.

For short fiction, the first notable work remains Esteban Echeverría's "El matadero." Apart from its importance as a first, it is exceptional as a representative of the general literary tendencies that would dominate much of Latin American writing until the decade of the 1880s, and to some extent, even after the renovative movement of that decade. For this reason, before considering the famous Argentine work, it would be well to look briefly at the "isms" it displays as well as particular manifestations of Latin American literature.

It may initially be startling to think of Echeverría, born in 1805, as a pioneer figure in Latin American romanticism. Readers accustomed to the European literary chronology tend to place ths movement at the end of the eighteenth century with some overlap into the nineteenth; however, romanticism did not have an opportunity to develop in Spanish-speaking countries until well into the latter century. The fashionable young Echeverría acquired his romantic tendencies at the source, making the pilgrimage to Paris that would become virtually obligatory for youthful Latin American innovators; by the 1830s he was producing romantic literature in Spanish and promoting the new mode in Buenos Aires intellectual circles. One might add that Echeverría's French-imported romanticism would soon be supplemented by other strains derived from the Spanish peninsula and other sources; the new fusion produced in Latin America would outlive the European forms of the movement by many years.

Romanticism was certainly the mode to which Echeverría devoted the closest study. In "Matadero," though, he supplemented romantic elements with passages much more indicative of incipient realism. This fusion, although not an exclusively Latin American phenomenon, is seen in many of that continent's nineteenth-century works. Writers, eager to speak out on issues of national destiny, were irresistibly attracted to the flamboyant and striking rhetoric of romanticism, an elevated style that seems to have taken an especially strong hold of Spanish literary language. This did not mitigate the strong desire to render with detailed vividness scenes of barbarism, misery, or exotic appeal, however.

In the ideas it expresses, Echeverría's writing is identifiable with the rationalistic enlightenment. He exemplified the young Latin American intellectual who, regarding his country as a locus of savagery, sought a reformation of national life through application of the precepts of French eighteenth-century rationalism. While a great deal could be said about the ideas connected with the enlightenment, only a few are directly relevant to Echeverría's short story: the conviction that European civilization is more worthy than the rougher grass-roots cultures to what today would be called Third-World peoples; the desire to cast down tyrannical rulers and replace them with a logically programmed form of governance; and a general proclamation of the abstract virtues of truth, liberty, justice, and rational inquiry. Clearly, the elements Echeverría brought to the writing of his story were already in profound contradiction; the romantic idealization of wild and uncultivated humanity opposed the notion that more civilizing order was always a mark of progress.

As well as exemplifying realism and romanticism, "El Matadero" is representative of a phenomenon designated as *costumbrismo,* that is, careful observation and literary reproduction of the detailed texture of everyday life. This literary tendency is not explored fully in the case of

Echeverría, but postponed until the discussion of later writers who rely on *costumbrismo* as a more dominant mode in their writing.

A second issue that is not weighed here is whether "El Matadero" is truly a short story. In practice, this controversy is generally resolved by treating it as such. For example, Carlos Mastrángelo has made the strongest argument against considering the work as a short story, pointing out its lack of unity. Yet he is obliged to include discussion of it in his 1975 *El cuento argentino* (The Argentine Short Story) even as he denies it a place in the genre, simply because of the work's importance. A further impediment to complete resolution of the problem is the fact that Echeverría did not publish the text during his lifetime. No one is certain whether the version he left was a definitive one or was a preliminary effort intended to be expanded or edited to a more recognizable generic form.

"El Matadero" begins with an extended passage of highly rhetorical and sarcastic speech-making on the part of the narrator. In language of mock-biblical elevation, he sets forth the situation to be developed. Despite his elaborate mode of expression, the targets of his attack are clearly distinguished. They are those institutional powers that benefit from manipulation of the barbaric drives of the uneducated masses. The exploitative forces that follow this plan are identified primarily as populist demagogy (clearly, the antiintellectual regime of Juan Manuel Rosas, responsible for suppressing the activities of Echeverría and his generational cohort of freethinkers) and secondarily the church that allied itself with such tyranny. The concrete case to be considered is an especially blatant "bread and circuses" tactic, a savage entertainment provided for the fanatically carnivorous residents of Buenos Aires. With brazen disregard for the lenten discipline of abstinence—it is Good Friday in the story—the authorities have allowed a great festival of slaughtering and distributing of beef cattle. In his perorations, the narrator points out how typical it is of both governmental and ecclesiastic strategy to appeal shamelessly to the basest drives of the people.

This opening, rather essayistic in its exposition, gives way to a more allegorical denunciation of Rosas and his supporters. Now the slaughter ground itself, with its masses of revelers, becomes a figure for the Argentine nation under Rosas's domination. With the establishment of this central metaphor, the narrator's editorial intervention recedes considerably. Such a shift from telling about to showing allows the elaboration of an impressive series of realistic descriptions.

This central portion of the work consists of vivid scenes of carnage and celebration. Echeverría spares no distressing detail, showing his rabble of characters in riotous jubilation amid gouts of blood, severed pieces of freshly slaughtered flesh, and the detritus of butchering. Throughout these chaotic scenes there is insistence on the features common to both the revelers and Rosas's supporters. The crowd is composed of the very elements of the population that Rosas most assiduously courted: not only the poor, but specifically the partly Indian gauchos, the black, and the mulatto groups (an unfortunate link is made between non-European ancestry and barbarism). The extreme brutality and callousness of these manipulable masses is manifest in several episodes. The meat-crazed crowd hurls hunks of beef through the air, fails to register proper shock at the accidental slitting of a child's throat, and glories in the growing profusion of mangled animal matter. Such behavior is a reminder of the bloodiness, cruelty, and lack of any human refinement that Echeverría saw as the essentials of Rosism.

Opposition to this society of savagery comes through two figures. The first is a magnificent bull, explicitly identified by the narrator as displaying the spirit of a Unitarian (an opponent of Rosas). The creature appears only briefly as a sign of dignified resistance before being vanquished. In an evidently symbolic emasculation of anti-Rosas opposition, the masses castrate the defiant bull and make a sport of brandishing its severed testicles.

The second opposing figure is that of a young man who rides into the slaughter area. The crowd reacts wth hostility to the stranger's European riding gear and his refined presence. The detail is significant, since Rosas's populism stipulated rejection of European culture and a championing of gaucho-style dress, horsemanship, and bearing. The Europeanized youth quickly becomes the object of taunts, jostlings, and finally torture. Christologic symbology appears throughout this episode, with the tormented youth dying as if spread on a cross. Curiously, the man is not directly killed by his captors, but rather appears to rupture some major vessel during his anguished and futile thrashings. The manner of his death might be read as the enlightened, educated group dying of its own impotent frustration in the face of such massive savagery. This interpretation would correspond well with the actual situation of Echeverría and his intellectual elite, who had seen their associations disbanded, their political expression proscribed, and their continued presence in Argentina made impossible. The story ends with the narrator once more making pronouncements concerning the need for a new order based on respect for civilized values.

Powerful as its description may be, Echeverría's work is full of troubling contradictions. These difficulties are apparent when one attempts to consider the text as romantic writing. Romanticism is present in the ardent, flamboyantly metaphoric speech of the narrator. He reiterates biblical allusions and sarcastically interjects, "What nobility of spirit! What courage on the part of the Rosas mob! Always ganging up like vultures on their helpless prey." Scenes of torment alternate swiftly with editorializing or description of trivial events, providing the extremely variegated texture much favored by romantic colorists.

Seconding these romantic pleas for civilization are the realistically presented "proofs," the fictional pseudodocumentation of the evils of savage governance. It would be unfair to disqualify Echeverría as a romantic for his use of realistic description; the two tendencies are not necessarily incompatible. There were solid precedents for such a fusion. One of Echeverría's heroes, the Spanish writer Mariano José de Larra, was an able synthesizer of acute social observation with more lyrical passages commenting emotively on the phenomena described.

Where Echeverría's romanticism does falter is in his attitude toward the common people. European romanticism demanded from adherents an admiration for the life and artistic expression of the peasant. Sophisticated writers regularly claimed to be relearning their art at the feet of village tale-tellers and balladeers. Jean-Jacques Rousseau's exaltation of the noble savage, unblemished by the perverse refinements of modern Western culture, took many forms, based on folkloric and exotic paradigms.

Echeverría was able to share the enthusiasm for European peasant art to the point of producing a number of ballads in traditional European patterns. When it came to the peasants of his own continent, his admiration stopped. In Argentina, the "people" were Indians and gauchos, along with a black population then present in Buenos Aires. For Echeverría and for others of his intellectual generation, these groups were impediments to the establishment of rational programs for the national future. Rosas's appeal to these sectors only showed how low the dictator would stoop for support. The idea of including non-European ethnicities in national decision making was never considered; nor would the elite see itself as having much to learn from the cultures of such groups. The educated sector had had little opportunity to be surfeited with modern progress and felt no nostalgia for a more primitive way of life or an unclouded ignorance of urban ways.

The contradiction exemplified in "El Matadero" has both a literary and a social dimension. On the one hand, it calls into question the existence of any classically romantic movement in Latin America. While many texts exhibit Echeverría's attitudes toward Indians and gauchos, it is difficult to find examples of an informed appreciation of indigenous cultures. Even those writings that attempt a noble savage bias tend to lean heavily on the European model provided by René de Chateaubriand's 1801 *Atala,* a sentimental and stylized treatment of a culture perceived as exotic. Of Echeverría's generation, only Domingo Faustino Sarmiento seemed willing to glorify the gaucho for his romantically wild and free life; but he too saw this poetic culture as a useless anachronism.

This set of attitudes, consistently pro-European and antiindigenous, has importance in the development of national policy. Echeverría and his colleagues saw themselves as the shapers of post-Rosas Argentina, and wrote with this role in mind. Although Echeverría died in exile, the proscribed intellectuals who returned after Rosas's fall did implement a progressive program. Their project proved most beneficial to economic growth and the flowering of an elite culture, but these goals were achieved partly through the sacrifice of non-European cultures. The Indians were exterminated in the late 1880s; blacks largely disappeared because of tuberculosis; those of mixed Indian and Hispanic ancestry figure today among the urban underclass. Essayists who question the priorities set during Argentina's national formation (the so-called historical revisionists) have expressed considerable uneasiness at the type of social thought represented by "El Matadero."

Although signs of elitism and racism are abundant in writings of this period, it would be too great a generalization to consider these as invariable patterns. Throughout the period when authors were intent on forming and guiding a new society, concern was sporadically expressed for the indigenous population. A writer who manifested this preoccupation in the form of short fiction was the Ecuadorean Juan Montalvo (1832–1889).

Like Echeverría and his generation, Montalvo wrote against the backwardness and tyranny personified by a particular ruler. In his case, the dictator was Gabriel García Moreno, who during the 1860s and until 1875 ran Ecuador under a system of extreme repression coupled with continual invocation of church authority. As a countermodel to this elaborately tyrannical system with its combination of cultural pressures and ecclesiastic and governmental powers, Montalvo advocated a much simpler form of social order based largely on the citizenry's inherent altruism. He developed a humanistic Christian perspective, more concerned with general moral sensitivity than with strict formulations and codes. For the leadership of this new society, Montalvo foresaw a natural elite formed of individuals distinguished for their nobility of mind and spirit, their charity and vision. While this lofty rhetoric was common enough among educated liberals, Montalvo was unusual in his willingness to include the country's Indians in this intellectual and moral elite. At the same time, he admitted that the current state of the Indians, impoverished and demoralized by continued exploitation, did not make them likely candidates for the country's spiritual leadership.

Montalvo was principally an essayist, but he also chose to disseminate his ideas through the writing of entertaining fictions. For this purpose, he contrived further adventures for the universally familiar figures of Don Quixote and Sancho Panza. The resulting tales are an odd mixture of period-piece literature and digressive essays. The author's interest in the age of Cervantes led him to attempt a complex mimicry of Cervantes' prose style, complete with archaic linguistic features. Although the fictional elements are not very well integrated with the excursions into philosophy and national development, the posthumous collection *Capítulos que se le olvidaron a Cervantes* (1895; Chapters Cervantes Forgot), which appeared sporadically throughout the 1870s and 1880s, are of interest for antiquarian reasons as well as for their ideas. Montalvo was a somewhat cautious and abstract liberal, but his insistence on incorporating the Indian into national life was potentially radical in its implications. For this reason, he is considered the milder predecessor of such bold social essayists as Manuel González Prada (1848–1918) and José Carlos Mariátegui (1895–1930), both of whom were concerned with the need to recognize Peru as a nation with strong indigenous components in its identity structure. This very productive tradition of social criticism continues to the present, and includes such essential figures as the Salazar Bondy brothers (Sebastián, 1924–1965, and Augusto, 1925–   ), Alberto Escobar (1929–   ), and Julio Ortega (1942–   ).

If Montalvo was representative of topics that would be developed by later writers, he was also a typical exponent of a kind of literary language that would be rejected by these same authors. Montalvo was abstract, with a propensity for philosophizing at length about Justice and Virtue. His language was embellished with archaic flourishes. The massive effort to move away from this unwieldy literary standard was a major tenet of the modernist esthetic.

The Remaking of a Literary Language

Ricardo Palma (1833–1919), one of the most widely read of Peruvian authors, is also one of the most variously construed. Disparate critical opinions characterize this individualistic romantic as a folksy humorist, an astute social satirist, an innovative refashioner of literary Spanish, and a dangerous misrepresenter of Peru's national past.

To begin to characterize Palma one might well start with the most evident feature of his work. He invented his own personal literary genre, which he called the *tradición*. This short narrative form was not, in most cases, altogether of the author's invention. With his strong interest in the tradition of oral narrative, Palma gathered a vast amount of material ranging from widely circulated jokes to complete folk tales. He was also a devoted student of the history of Lima, particularly the colonial period, and sought out all types of anecdotes about the city without much regard for their historical veracity. This mass of picturesque information became the raw material of the *tradiciones*. Although the story lines were found rather than made, Palma was no literal transcriber in the manner of the Brothers Grimm. He allowed himself a high degree of artistic intervention, restructuring his anecdotes, adding further elaboration, and conflating various stories into one complicated new unit. This set of circumstances led Enrique Anderson Imbert to remark, "There is not a single virtue of the short story writer that Palma did not have. . . . But there is not a single 'tradition' that is really a short story."[1] Palma is generally regarded as a short story writer, however, and extensively anthologized as such because his treatment of collected anecdotes produced unified, carefully developed brief narratives, more the work of an artist than an oral historian.

A continuing issue in the discussion of Palma's work is identification of the values that it reflects, particualrly with respect to institutionalized power figures. Beyond any doubt, Palma was fascinated by the strategies through which both civil and ecclesiastic authority was exercised. Situating numerous *tradiciones* in the period when Lima was a vital center of Spanish colonial governance, Palma portrays a Byzantine network of governmental office holders, clergy, military men, and *hidalgos,* those well-born persons who could invoke privileges of rank.

The question that then arises is how this hierarchical colonial world is viewed—with fondness or with indignation. The most ardent proponent of the former was Sebastián Salazar Bondy, whose polemic essay "Lima la horrible" (1964; Lima the Horrible), painted Palma as a nostalgic admirer of the Spanish colonial world. According to this line of thought, the *tradiciones* are loved because of their creation of a harmoniously organized and homogeneously Hispanic-Catholic, *criollo,* population. The reader of the *tradiciones* is allowed to dismiss the most troubling aspect of Peru's history, the dispossession of the Indians and subsequent failure to make a place for this culturally disrupted group. It should be noted that Sebastián Salazar Bondy was concerned not only with Palma's texts themselves, but with enshrinement of the *tradiciones* as items of official culture.

This type of criticism is still common, however, Palma's treatment of the colonial period has strong defenders, the most celebrated being perhaps José Carlos Mariátegui in his 1928 *Siete ensayos de interpretación de la realidad peruana* (Seven Interpretive Essays on Peruvian Reality). Mariátegui cannot claim for Palma the rigorous socialist analysis to which colonial society should, according to his line of thought, be subjected. Yet he sees Palma as one of the least romantic and sentimental of authors to treat this epoch.

While one cannot deny the nostalgic note in the *tradiciones,* it is possible to see in them more than a loving re-creation of past times. Palma's critical and antiauthoritarian mode is most apparent when one considers the *tradiciones* quite apart from the aura of official approval surrounding them. His case is similar, in this respect, to that of Mark Twain. As presented in textbooks and popular films, Twain's works may seem mildly celebratory of Midwestern United States, but his subtly subversive satire can be appreciated by a reader not convinced of Twain's essential blandness.

A good case can be made for Palma as a writer capable of questioning and dismantling the patterns of traditional authority. The most manifest of his disarming strategies is simple caricature as seen in the many corrupt clergy members and underhanded officials who appear throughout the *tradiciones,* blustering, striking deals, practicing the art of intimidation, and indulging in the pleasures they publicly condemn. On a more covert level, Palma's subversive nature finds an outlet in subtle linguistic strategies that tend to identify and mock the weakest points in contemporary society. This use of language as sly lampooning occurs both in the speech of the characters—Palma is an excellent mimic of arrogant and sanctimonious language—and in the comments of the narrator, a wry observer of human misbehavior. If one takes this view of Palma's writing, he would appear to be drawn to the colonial *criollo* past precisely in search of a rigid and stratified social order ripe for satiric deflation.

The continuing discussion over the true nature of Palma's social vision is in itself testimony to the new artistic detachment the writer pioneered. The *tradiciones* are very distant from works like "El Matadero" or Montalvo's Don Quixote stories, from which the reader may abstract a rationale for identifying and solving national problems. Palma has no one program, but rather strikes a variety of attitudes determined by the particular narrative and its exigencies. Such emphasis on the artistic text itself, along with Palma's conscious development of literary language, makes him a transitional writer on the way to the modernist movement, with its insistence on the primacy of esthetic considerations.

"Pasquín y contrapasquín" (ca. 1892; "Broadside and Counter-Broadside") is representative of Palma's playful variety and fascination with the colonial era. The *pasquín* of the title is a medium of communication that flourished in earlier times in Hispanic countries. It consisted of a poster bearing a grave insult to a local person. The demeaning message, though, had to be displayed with style: scurrilous doggerel was ideal for the purpose. The *pasquín* would be widely posted overnight, casting aspersions on the target's competence, ancestry, legitimacy, honesty, or his wife's fidelity. Half serious communication and half frivolity, the *pasquín* campaign still lends itself well to fictional treatment as used by more widely recognized Latin American writers including Gabriel García Márquez (Colombia) and Augusto Roa Bastos (Paraguay).

Palma's narrator is, as usual, a wry individual who presents himself as no more than a reteller of absorbing anecdotes. A lengthy and digressive introduction to the story moves it out of the realm of the strictly historical and into the area of savored hearsay. The element that most undermines the historicity of the tale is a basic uncertainty as to the identity of the Viceroy involved, whether of Lima or of Mexico. The narrator provides information about the hereditary titles of both, and about their respective positions in the Spanish imperial hierarchy, an intricate matter. While this listing of honors might give the impression of an author enraptured with the elite, the subsequently provided background information casts these noble gentlemen in a less favorable light. The Peruvian Viceroy is famous for having ordered the beheading of two citizens simply because he heard they were frequent brawlers. This information gives an ironic shading to the earlier respectful allusions to the "most excellent gentlemen."

The following passages center on evidence of the arbitrary nature of colonial rule. Working always with hearsay, the narrator reports the Viceroy to be a capricious tyrant who "on a day he got out of bed on the wrong side" might easily order "just over breakfast" the death by hanging of the most upstanding of subjects. In a typically Palma-style digression, the narrator brings together various pieces of anecdotal material and displays a maximum number of colorful and memorable flourishes of period language. This mass of diverse components is unified by a desire to expose the random violence that any man in the Viceroy's position could exercise. This background section ends with a different Viceroy's quoted remark on personally murdering a subordinate: "I don't care for all this legal-eagle business and paper-pushing, I just grab my knife and set things straight; *bad vinegar or good sherry, I don't care what the deal is.*" The coarse expression used by the colonial official, as well as his brutal outlook, reflect on the quality of individual often elevated to the position of King's representative.

The core anecdote concerning *pasquines* is embedded in this considerable mass of apparently digressive material. Yet the preliminaries set the story in context by stressing the nature of colonial authority—not just one Viceroy's behavior, but that of at least three arrogant tyrants in this post. The first *pasquín* to appear is a direct questioning of the legitimacy of this authority. The anonymous versifier addresses the Viceroy in an open letter, telling him, "You don't look like anybody's your Excellency / you don't dress like a Viceroy," and goes on to suggest that the Viceroy is a living affront to both human and divine law. The narrator clearly savors this antiauthoritarian doggerel, gloating, "What an insolent *pasquín!*"

The twist that completes the anecdote is the posting of a counter-*pasquín* by the outraged official. This counterattack is not in the spirit of the anarchic *pasquín,* but simply uses the medium for authoritarian purposes. The Viceroy reminds his subjects that however they may judge his appearance, "I represent the King and I possess his omnipotence." Wasting no space on humorous sallies, the official threatens with decapitation any citizen found engaged in such subversive tactics.

As the narrator subsequently informs the reader, the counter-*pasquín* effectively squelched all impulse to make sport of the Viceroy and his mode of governance.

As one may gather, the interest of much nineteenth-century Latin American fiction lies not so much in its romanticism as in the authors' ability to fuse elements of the movement with other tendencies. Such a generalization certainly is applicable to the prolific Mexican writer Manuel Payno. This popular author, who lived from 1810–1894, produced a large body of purely romantic fiction, both short stories and longer narratives, which is now chiefly of historical interest. Payno remains known for quite a different type of short story, the action-filled series *Los bandidos de Río Frío* (1889–1899; The Bandits of Río Frío). These tales, very much in the swashbuckling tradition, combine the narrator's markedly romantic and melodramatic rhetoric with close observation and recording of daily existence in the Mexican provinces.

A few other romantic figures are of interest today chiefly because of the great appeal they exercised on contemporary reading publics. The Mexicans Vincente Riva Palacio (1832–1896) and Juan Sierra O'Reilly (1814–1861), and the Argentine Vicente Fidel López (1815–1903) were all adept at romanticizing and elaborating an historical event including many turns of plot: coincidences, rescues, and the treachery of cruel villains. The great vogue of writers such as Sir Walter Scott and René de Chateaubriand was certainly stimulating to Latin American fiction. As has often been pointed out, however, the fascination with tales of adventure distracted writers from the work of finding specifically Latin American modes of literary presentation capable of reflecting the realities of the New World.

Realism and Naturalism

Early realism routinely tended to become mixed with romantic elements, and nowhere more than in depiction of rural, poor, and indigenous characters. Whatever value might be assigned to native culture, from chronic nuisance to splendid anachronism, authors were consistently drawn to the creation of larger-than-life, striking, and exotic figures of uncivilized humankind. The advent of naturalism brought a rejection of such romanticizing. The new ideal was to transcribe reality with clinical objectivity, sparing the reader neither the banality nor the horror of everyday life.

While one might expect a more accurate and just representation of indigenous groups to result from abandonment of the "thrilling savages" stereotype, naturalist authors, too, were responsible for diffusing some prejudicial notions about these marginal populations. Perhaps the most exemplary practitioner of this rural naturalism, as well as a skillful and self-conscious literary craftsman, was the Uruguayan Javier de Viana (1868–1926).

Several features make Viana a typical naturalist: his inclusion of clinical data (this was the heyday of physician-authors, including Eduardo Wilde [1844–1913], Francisco Sicardi, [1856–1927], and Manuel Podestá, [1853–1920] in Argentina), his focusing on a particular social milieu, and his extensive field experience reflected in detailed reportorial description. Like other progressive thinkers of his time, Viana had read the most important French authors, Emile Zola and Guy de Maupassant, as well as absorbed currently fashionable ideas about the alleged degeneracy of certain racial stocks. Viana was a concerned and educated observer who would today be considered paternalistic and somewhat racist.

His chosen object of study, to use the naturalists' quasi-scientific terminology, was the gaucho population of the Argentine and Uruguayan plains. This group of racially mixed herdsmen, long alienated both from indigenous and Hispanic cultures, had acquired a powerful outcast mystique. Rejecting this romantic image, Viana presented the plains people as a typical rural marginal population. While the myth tended to emphasize the gaucho's resistance to the trivial constraints of civilization, making of the group an emblem of embattled independence, Viana presented a picture of an isolated, chaotic, and brutal society. Rejection of modern social regulation and material improvements was seen not as an expression of proud anarchism, but as the sign of apathetic, degenerate laxity. In accord with the genetic determinism then in vogue, Viana believed that the plains dwellers represented a deteriorated strain of humankind incapable of organized self-improvement.

This thorough demythification of the gaucho is evident in "La tísica" (1905; The Consumptive). The narrator of this short story is a rationalistic and well-meaning doctor; the principal drama lies in the liberal gentleman's encounter with phenomena resistent to reasonable and benevolent treatment.

While many writers have attested to the brutalizing quality of a given milieu, Viana is often able to distinguish his stories with some structural feature that provides greater complexity. In "La tísica," this twist is provided through the point of view of a highly involved, ambiguous, first-person narrator. The articulate, compassionate man is the very type of civilized individual Viana would like to see enlighten the backlands. Yet he is far from achieving a clear view of the gaucho's situation and freely admits to being horrified and confused by his experiences in the provinces. In trying to account for his failure to establish communication with the local people, the doctor places issues of discourse and comprehensibility in the foreground.

In the first portion of the story, the doctor presents himself as a humanistic and rationalistic progressive, eager to defend the town pariah against primitive scapegoating. He thus becomes the champion of the frail, docile young woman generally believed to be possessed of a malign spirit. To the urban medical man, the matter appears to be a simple case of persecution mania. He recalls the fervor with which he would seek to engage the locals in rational conversation and reason them out of their jeering cruelty toward the woman; these efforts prove singularly futile as the rurals can only reply to the doctor's arguments with simple metaphors likening her to a scorpion or other dangerous animal. This magically analogic way of treating the issue disgusts the man influenced by positivist thought.

Moreover, the doctor himself would seem to be doing a fairly poor job of thinking about the young woman. As he brushes aside the country people's animal metaphors, he also disregards the one piece of verifiable information about her: all the animals she cares for die. To explain this uncomfortable fact, the doctor indulges in what appears to be for him a curiously illogical turn of language when he attributes the animals' deaths to some force comparable to "an evil spell." He is as quick as the country people to think of the girl as an animal, although his figure for her is that of a shy, silky-haired burrowing animal.

The misunderstanding and frustration on both sides grows until it climaxes in a chaotic exchange between the doctor and a countryman. The educated man insists on an explanation for the obvious terror the woman evokes. Pressed for an explanation, the local can give none; his baffled response shows his inability to understand why any explanation should be demanded for a situation that simply is "that way."

A surprise twist ends the story: the doctor's later discovery that the woman whose innocent goodness he proclaimed was, in fact, a psychotic killer. The fact that the unreasoning country people were right and the representative of science was wrong underscores again the extreme

difficulty that educated city people face in dealing with the rural population. The doctor has been unable not only to converse with the people
but even to read the signs of everday country life. This ending sounds a
thoroughly disheartening note, for the new information reveals the
immensity of the gulf between the wretched, degenerate gauchos and
those who would attempt to reach and assist them.

As one may imagine, Viana's type of naturalism may prove uncomfortable to present-day readers. He calls for a new awareness of the
gauchos' problems and a new willingness to provide guidance. Yet with
his scientific distancing and insistence on the animal characteristics of
human beings, he renders the beleaguered population repulsive. The
group is not given credit for any capacity for self-direction or for any
valuable cultural traits. Whether associated metaphorically with de-
spised animals such as scorpions or poisonous snakes, or with prized
ones (as in the case of the burrowing creatures of the pampas to which
he compares the girl), the gaucho figuratively loses human status. Such
insistence on the degeneration of indigenous and semi-indigenous
peoples was eventually to produce a counterreaction among later
writers. To balance the picture, fiction writers such as Rosario Castellanos (Mexico, 1925–1974) and José María Arguedas (Peru, 1911–
1969) stress the rich interior lives and imaginative culture of Indian
characters.

The naturalistic traits of scientism (or, as the case may be, pseu-
doscientific theorizing) and extreme detachment from their wretched
characters are less evident in the work of the Chilean Baldomero Lillo
(1867–1923). Sometimes called a naturalist for his grim, detailed scenes
of human degradation, Lillo avoids many of the presuppositions often
associated with that movement. He does not seek to attribute apathy
and unprogressive attitudes to racial deterioration, poor heredity, or
other organic causes. His characters are wretched for reasons that
would make any human being miserable: poor housing, exploitation of
labor, and intolerable working conditions. While Viana's naturalism
suggests a deterioration so massive that one can scarecely begin to
remedy it, Lillo points toward specific reforms that must be undertaken.
Also unlike Viana's alienating effects are Lillo's efforts to engage the
reader's human sympathies for the suffering of his characters. For these
reasons, Lillo's work is not clearly classifiable as naturalistic.

Like Viana, Lillo chooses a special population as the object of his
literary inquiry; however, the group is not defined by hereditary traits or
non-European cultural characteristics. Common features are harsh

working conditions, lack of education, and a precarious economic existence. Mining communities are the most frequent settings in his short story collections *Sub terra* (1904, Below Ground) and *Sub sole* (1907, Sub Surface).

Lillo was interested both in the denunciation of specific problems and in the more general task of depicting life among the hard-pressed miners' families. A story that shows Lillo's interest in the rural poor as human beings is "El pozo" (The Well) from the 1904 collection. "El pozo" is principally a personal chronicle of conflicting passions, but contains constant references to the social background that helped shape the characters' often rough and brutal behavior.

The beginning passages highlight the tale of individual emotions and conflicts. With language that emphasizes the hot-blooded and excitable natures of the protagonists, the narrator introduces a village belle and her rival suitors. In swift order, the heroine repels one ardent young man's proposal of marriage, finds herself obliged to fight off his forceful advances, and is rescued by the favored rival. In these events, elements of reckless violence and uncontrolled excitement predominate; the losing suitor has "dark eyes full of fire" and is "drunk with spite and desire." The rivalry climaxes in a fight so unrestrained that the enemies inadvertently lay waste to a valuable garden.

This series of events ushers in some contrasting passages designed to turn the reader's attention from the explosive young people and toward the social milieu. The heroine's home is described in characteristically unappetizing realistic detail, complete with descriptions of a layer of malodorous filth on the floor, and the mother's face, blotched with age and hard living. Lillo's narrator often surveys a scene with the eye of a hygiene-and-safety-inspector; here, he comments on the facilities for washing and the odd bits of refuse in corners.

The previously related events, already told as part of a chaotic love story, are now seen as happenings that affect the community's life. The damage the heedless young men have caused to the community's food resources is discovered and becomes the occasion for communal wailing and cursing. This scene of shared distress, which closes the first segment of the story, underscores the idea that these economically vulnerable people, especially given to wild, irrational outbursts, are those who can least afford the luxury of letting go in this way.

The narrator continues to stress the inseparability of community and personal events and the reckless irrationality of the young protagonists' actions. Characteristically, he addresses the reader to explain the underlying causes of the events he is describing. In analyzing the disturbed relations among the three protagonists, the narrator makes a special point of their having acted instinctively, and notes their inability to comprehend their own motivations. There is strong and explicit emphasis on the country people's lack of insight into their own actions and their habitual domination by instinctual drives. Frankly judgmental, the narrator establishes his identity as a rationalist eager to see human beings live in a reflective and ordered manner. He is clearly appalled by the disorderly way in which members of the unstable triangle play out their emotions.

This editorializing section, besides constituting a typical example of traditional realistic narration, shows the difference between Lillo's treatment of his impoverished subjects and the more alienating and distancing work of, for example, Viana. Viana's characters seem so unlike the modern urbane reader that they fail to provoke much sympathy. A story like "La Tísica" carries the message that educated city people can scarcely understand what is happening among the savage portions of their own country's populations. In contrast, Lillo strongly makes the point that educated readers can understand the feelings and actions of seemingly barbaric country people. The characters' wildness stems from perfectly comprehensible natural urges that need only a certain amount of analysis (supplied by the scientific-sounding narrator) to be perceived by an outside observer. Unlike Viana's dirty, unhealthy characters, repulsive to the reader, Lillo's three protagonists are fairly bursting with health, natural beauty, and high spirits. The analytic commentary on their situation makes it clear that what they lack is a system of rational and "civilized" constraints in their altogether human passion and exuberance.

Following this editorializing interlude, Lillo continues the vivid scenes of action for which he is best remembered. The most impressive of these describes one of the rival's entrapment and suffocation in a dry well. Lillo here has incorporated many details designed to augment the reader's feeling of horror. The narrator shifts from conveying the perceptions and reactions of the trapped man to relating the response of the community members gathered around the scene. Carefully he describes the doomed man's panicky cries from the well, his mother's frenzied actions on the surface, and the townspeople's helpless and confused efforts to assist. An upsetting ironic dimension comes from the fact that the well's collapse is actually occasioned when the concerned community gathers around it to help the trapped young man. The weight of the crowd on the surrounding sandy soil triggers the cave-in, a circumstance the trapped man's enemy had counted on to destroy his rival. Only the reader and a few of the more astute townspeople are aware of the negative effects of the rescue efforts, and observe with dismay the well-meaning crowd's continued inadvertent destruction of the well's unstable walls. The readers's complete grasp of the situation, contrasted with the ignorant characters' unthinking actions, creates a significant tension, underlining again the need to remake the rural Chilean in a more reflective and rationalistic mold.

Even more direct denunciation of material conditions is central to "La compuerta Número 12" (Gate Number 12) from the same volume. This story is famous for a scene in which a miner must introduce his terrified son into the mines to begin what will be his lifelong work. "La Compuerta Número 12" exhibits many of the same features as "El Pozo," that is, a general evocation of harsh living conditions, economic vulnerability, and unthinking expression of feelings. The climactic horrible scene is, nevertheless more directly aimed at working conditions in need of reform and regulation, with the reader encouraged to identify with the grief of the family that must force its child into a life of degradation. In the climactic scene, there is a vigorous effort to convey the terror of the child. Having finally grasped the purpose of his trip to the mines, he panics and is tied by his own father to a rock deep underground. The father, equally distraught but constrained by the need for economic survival, hacks at the hard coal in such a frenzy that the air is filled with flying coal fragments. This scene, with its gruesome detailing of the child's frantic pleading, the coal shards lodging in the father's flesh, and the thick accumulation of coal dust and splinters in the air, is probably the most famous of Lillo's many descriptions of catastrophic and traumatic events.

Successful as Lillo's work was in exciting sympathy for the plight of miners and their families, it also displays some of the characteristics that would later be rejected by postrealist writers. Principal among these is the high degree of intervention of the narrator. The portion of "El pozo" in which the narrator comments on the hidden motives of the protagonists' passionate behavior is typical. The narrator is not only omniscient in the sense of having complete access to the characters' consciousness, he is a universally knowledgeable expert capable of explaining all matters with the scientific tools of psychologic and sociologic analysis.

Because of the development of newer modes of *indigenista* writing, these earlier works concerning Indian life are likely to appear at something of a disadvantage. There is perhaps a reasonable tendency to assume that writers of the nineteenth and early twentieth centuries, however concerned over the Indians' plight, did not fully recognize them as human beings with a rich heritage of personal and cultural experiences. Such a generalization is not altogether applicable to the short stories of Enrique López Albújar (Peru, 1872–1966). A rural judge for many years, López Albújar had an interest in the organization of concepts of justice and their pragmatic administration among Peruvian Indians. A typical story might tell of a crime with major emphasis on the indigenous community's reaction and eventual resolution of the disruption of social order. López Albújar's work may seem dated or less than literary because of its heavy editorializing and endlessly authoritative narrative voice. Still, it makes more of a point than do many contemporary writings of the Indians' complex social organization and their ability to apply abstract concepts to concrete problems of justice. This feature sets López Albújar apart from writers who were only interested in the Indian as a victim of social sins worthy of denunciation. The stories are collected in *Cuentos andinos* (1920; Andean Stories), and *Nuevos cuentos andinos* (1937; New Andean Stories).

Costumbrismo

Concurrent with these grim forms of realistic fiction were others less harrowing to read. An often light-hearted variant of realism became known in Spanish-speaking countries as *costumbrismo*. This designation arises from the authors' close observation and recording of the social customs of a given group. The *costumbrista* author was an attentive student of everyday life, registering the small patterns that gave even routine interactions a distinctive stamp. In Spain, writers such as Ramón Mesonero Romanos gave the Madrid public vignettes of their own most typical behavior. *Costumbrismo* also provided educated urban readers with a glimpse of daily existence in isolated regions or in exotic subcultures. This latter type of work became especially common in Latin American countries. Well-off readers, whose direct contact with rural and peasant cultures was likely to be minimal, were nonetheless interested in literary representations of these phenomena.

Among Latin American writers, *costumbrismo* manifested itself in both trivially precious local-color sketches and in purposefully designed literary works. "El matadero," for instance, draws on this source;

but so do many tedious stories about village dances, rodeos, mountain vistas, and tales told around the fire. Writers who stand out for their mastery of amusing and yet significant short stories of social observation are Tomás Carrasquilla (Colombia, 1858–1940), José López Portillo y Rojas (Mexico, 1850–1923), Ignacio M. Altamirano (Mexico, 1834–1893), and Roberto J. Payró (Argentina, 1867–1928). Payró is an excellent example of this group because his work so clearly exemplifies the problems faced by educated authors when writing about uneducated rural characters. Payró's stories are collected in *Pago Chico* (1910) and the posthumous *Nuevos cuentos de Pago Chico* (1961; New Tales of Pago Chico).

The community is representative of the small-town social order, with its personal and informal way of handling all matters. Payró shows it in the process of transition from this comfortable Gemeinschaft to regulation (or at least attempted regulation) by agents of centralized government. In the spirit of anarchic socialism, he shows this change as a fundamental error. The residents of Pago Chico are excitable and sometimes riotous, but they know their own needs better than the new administrators do.

"En la policía" (At the Police Station) carries this political vision by means of a brief country joke. An inspector sent by the new, vigorous supervisory structure, shows up in Pago Chico and encounters the greatest difficulty in contacting the proper authorities. After some confusion, he is attended by a courteous man who answers the police-station door and responds to the inspector's questions. This man turns out to be the town prisoner. The commissioner, a typical example of backwoods laxity, has failed to hire any subordinates but has himself kept the funds provided for this purpose. He is currently in a back room, sleeping off a drunken spree under the supervision of the prisoner.

Besides its denunciation of administrative corruption, the story contains a more complex sociopolitical commentary. Although it does not function in the style of a city government, Pago Chico is still well run. Order is maintained by the prisoner's clearly defined sense of his role in the town and by his uncoerced willingness to help out. The story is one of several in which Payró shows the small town's ability to maintain order, not by any careful regulation, but by the ability to work out ad hoc solutions to its problems. Relying on face-to-face dealings and personal knowledge of the situation, they have no need for a bureaucratic society.

"El diablo en Pago Chico" (The Devil in Pago Chico), a longer, more representative story, like many Pago Chico stories, contains a great deal of descriptive material provided by an omniscient third-person narrator. This is the feature that has proved most problematic in Payró's attempts to show literary sympathy to the common people of the countryside.

Long before the narrator introduces his characters, he has set forth a very lengthy description of Pago Chico and its surrounding landscape. To some extent, this exercise in landscape-painting does reflect the concerns of the local people. As a countryman would, the narrator monitors the weather, the dryness of the vegetation, and the health of the livestock, matters a Pago Chico resident would necessarily perceive in the countryside because economic survival depends on awareness of them. By embellishing his prologue with a great many pictorial touches, however, the narrator sets himself apart from the local people. Describing the colors of the scene, the great sense of isolation, and the endlessness of the largely empty stretches of land, the narrator is remarking on phenomena more interesting to a literary observer than to a countryman. In this way, he seems to move both toward the common people, sharing their concerns over weather and stock, and away from them, toward an artistic delight in representing landscape.

The degree of detachment fluctuates continually throughout the story. In relating an encounter between a local family and a Frenchman passing through the community, the dialogue becomes much simpler and hence much closer to the characters. The emphasis is not on the narrator's skill at description but on the family's careful ritual of hospitality to a stranger. The same grass-roots unobstrusive narration continues as family members speculate on whether they have just entertained the devil.

The narrator has not abandoned the lyrical prose of the prologue, however. When a menacing, funnel-shaped duststorm approaches, he is the first to describe it: "The sky to the west was an immense cloak of purple, mirrored to the east in a flimsy veil, also purple-shaded. And in front of this veil an erect column of earth-laden dustclouds. . . ." This passage, so markedly the work of an individual trained in literary expression, stands oddly against the character's subsequent cry of "Hey! The twisters are starting up!" Throughout the narration of the duststorm and a catastrophic fire, there is continual contrast in the narrator's rhetorical level. When he describes actions taken by the characters, his language is relatively unadorned; the quotations from the characters are even more simple and direct. But when he turns his attention to the skies and landscape, there is a renewal of lyrical prose.

One must ask how much of a problem is presented by this linguistic fluctuation. After all, many works make striking use of varied speech patterns. In Payró's case, though, there is the troubling matter of the narrator's obvious expressive superiority over his humble characters, whose language is inevitably basic and concrete. Noé Jitrik has raised this issue with special reference to Payró's more humorous stories.[2] He finds the humor to reside in the gap between the narrator's mastery of fancy language and the plain characters on whom this elegant language is lavished. More generally, he is dissatisfied with the narrator's need to express himself in a language so much above that of the characters. To his mind, this problem is really a sign of a condescending attitude and a desire to remain detached from the experience of country simpletons.

Jitrik's complaint has some validity. In fact, it is possible to find even more direct evidence of Payró's occasional patronizing attitude, as when he speaks of characters' "childish superstition." It should nevertheless be pointed out that Payró was using the literary language and conventions available to him at that time. In adopting the point of view of a third-person narrator, he almost automatically assumed a more elevated language than that of his characters. In *El casamiento de Laucha* (1906; Laucha's Marriage), the fictional autobiography of a picaresque countryman, the problem does not arise. Thus one may say that the essential difficulty lies in the too-florid language of the narrator. The revolutionary changes that transformed Latin American narrative during the twentieth century would eventually lower the rhetorical level of this elevated expression.

Modernism

The last great "ism" in the development of nineteenth-century Latin American literature is modernism. Many tentative approaches to its definition have proved useful for various purposes, but the aspect most relevant to the present discussion is the movement's effort to renovate literary language in Spanish, although it should be noted that other critical discussions may emphasize other aspects of the phenomenon. Critics and readers interested in the history of ideas often read modernist writings with an eye to the philosophical notions derived from Arthur Schopenhauer (especially the concept of an unconscious driving will in the activities of the human species) and Victor Hugo (the role of the writer as a vatic seer or demigod).

Another common approach in delineating the movement is to examine the relations between European artistic schools, especially the French symbolists and parnassians, and the Latin American modernists, who synthesized ideas and techniques from various sources. The historians of Latin American modernism have also investigated the complex bonds between the movement and its Spanish equivalent. Still another line of inquiry follows the occult philosophy common to many modernists. This concern was especially important as a motivating force behind the vigorous linguistic innovations of the movement; there was a strong belief that elaboration of a poetically harmonious language could lead to great insights into the cosmic design.[3]

There is a long-standing tendency to think of modernism as a movement of poets. Recently, however, the parallel experimentation with literary prose has claimed fresh attention. The group's prose work has particular significance for readers attempting to identify the changes produced by modernism. Premodernist Spanish-language prose was clearly a language in need of reinvigoration. As the previous examples have shown, Latin American writers tended to focus their literary efforts on the pragmatic goal of spreading their social ideas. The language of speech-making and of literary expression comingled indiscriminately. No real thought had been given to the issue of developing a literary standard of expression that would be linguistically representative of the New World and designed to fulfill its particular needs. The modernists complained that existing literary Spanish was lacking in artistically balanced rhythmic patterns and overflowing with romantic stock phrases and conventional adjectives. The long reign of romantic and realistic models had exhausted the freshness these approaches might once have had.

The first great reworker of Latin American prose was the Cuban José Martí (1853–1895), best known to North Americans as the poet whose verse was put to song as the popular "Guantanamera." Martí stands somewhat apart from modernism as such because of his insistence on literature's social usefulness. Although Martí himself often strayed from this ideal, writing more for artistry than for diffusion of concepts, he censured his own work for this tendency toward the esthetic. Despite his vacillations, he never reached the art-for-art's-sake position typical of confirmed modernists. The idea of reserving a privileged space for artistically wrought language repelled him; literary language had to remain within the discourse of human affairs. What was modernistic in Martí was the close attention he paid to creating an esthetically satisfying verbal texture, whether in poetry, literary prose, or pamphleteering. He stressed the importance of language's rhythm—that is, the elaboration of phrases whose sound patterns would be harmonious and esthetically satisfying. Another much-needed reform was the avoidance of the overused adjectives of romanticism—pallid, somber, sweet, fragrant—and their replacement with a fresh and expanded supply of adjectives that could not be anticipated by the reader.

The greater part of Martí's prose was in the form of essays and even pamphlets. Martí felt the need for these more pragmatic modes because he was very directly involved with a real-world cause: the liberation of Cuba. During long periods of exile in the United States, he continued to meet with others concerned with ending Spanish domination of the island; eventually he died in a pro-Independence invasion force in 1895. Despite these pressing demands on his time, Martí wrote many reflective and imaginative pieces. An extremely inventive journalist, he specialized in what today might be called documentary literature, or new journalism. That is to say, he described contemporary events using the strategies and techniques of a skilled fiction writer. "El terremoto de Charleston" (1886; The Charleston Earthquake) is a fine example of this genre, with its narration of the community's horror and eventual recuperation from the castrophe. Martí also wrote more purely fictional prose, although his documentary reelaborations of events are most widely read.

Modernism began to take shape as a self-conscious group movement with the rise to prominence of the Nicaraguan Rubén Darío (1867–1916). Darío was a child prodigy of poetry and quickly attracted attention for his facility in elaborating quantities of patriotic, amorous, and occasional verse. The cultured elite were fascinated by this very young poet from such an improbable background (the backroads town of Metapa, Nicaragua, today named after its poet). He was soon a prized guest of prominent individuals and of governments. This early career pattern seemed to be turning Darío into a permanent court poet figure; however, while a houseguest of the President of Chile, the prodigy undertook a serious program of reading in his host's library. Access to recent developments in French literature sparked his interest in becoming a more innovative writer, but he certainly did not enlist in any one French literary movement. Rather, his practice was to absorb esthetic ideas from many sources without concerning himself with the differences between the rival "isms." Victor Hugo, Catulle Mendès, Théophile Gautier, and François Coppée were a somewhat disparate group of early influences, but Darío saw in them all alternatives to the traditional Hispanic modes he had already exhausted. This eclecticism of influence was to continue throughout his career, enabling the modernist group to use the impressionistic sensory-appeal imagery of the parnassians jointly with the abstract allusions of their rivals, the symbolists.

Darío's own debut as an experimental writer was his 1888 *Azul. . .* (Azure. . .). The author was apparently slow to apply his new esthetic program in verse, so that the prose sections of *Azul . . .* display the greatest degree of innovation. Among these are a decidedly naturalistic short story, "El Fardo" (The Load), several stories reflecting the author's newer and more experimental notions, and many non-generic prose fragments characterized by a predominance of sensory impressions.

"La muerte de la emperatriz de la China" ("The Death of the Empress of China"), is one of the more distinctively modern pieces in the volume. Unlike several other prose works, it does not reuse the romantic theme of the misunderstood artist in a heartless bourgeois world. There is more of the esthetic distancing associated with modernism. Although the events are disturbing to the characters, neither the narrator nor the reader is emotionally caught up in their drama. Instead, the characters are observed from without, and with more attention to the curious exoticism of their situation than to human dimension. The very topic, an artist's passionate obsession with a statue and his wife's jealous fury, lends itself particularly to this detached and playfully de-humanized treatment.

In line with the modernist ideal of cosmopolitanism, the story brings together unlike cultural references to create a fictional world of bizarre elegance. The basic setting is the artistic Bohemia of Paris, the city modernists held to be the epicenter of all esthetic movement. There is no attempt to depict realistically aspects of Bohemian life, however, and one gathers this particular setting was invoked only for its automatic associations of glamour and dashing unconventionality.

More specific than this general Parisian setting are allusions to Asian civilizations and their artifacts. The Oriental note is introduced through a character whose only personality trait seems to be an abnormally intense preoccupation with Far Eastern decorative articles—with japoiserie and chinoiserie, as the narrator puts it. In a passage exemplary of the modernist love of sensual exoticism, the narrator describes in some detail the marvelously intricate and curious items gathered by the obsessed collector.

Along with the French Bohemian and Oriental touches, the story uses an eclectic variety of allusions to build up the notion of a pervasive exoticism. The hero regards his wife as if she were H. Rider Haggard's Ayesha, the goddess-woman who dominates that writer's literarily embellished savage terrain. The woman's face is like "the hieratic profile of the medallion of a Byzantine empress." This acumulation of allusions is important in establishing that the characters are purely artistic creations inhabiting a special literary space unlike any real-world locale.

The events that unfold against this intricately decorative setting are simple and enigmatic. The hero's rapture over his friend's Chinese statue, which succeeds in alienating him from his wife, can be appreciated with or without interpretation. The triumph of the artistically created image over the flesh-and-blood woman is an easily identifiable correlate of Darío's championing of artifice over naturalistic or realistic representation. In addition, his willingness to dwell on this unnatural attachment is in itself a statement. Darío was experimenting with the literary figuration of sexuality. He was especially fascinated with the more sophisticated variants, and worked extensively with the idea that modern sexual attraction is often the creation of art, not simply a naturally occurring phenomenon. Throughout his work, one finds women whose allure is a triumph of art: stylishly seductive behaviors, complicated dress, and sumptuous surroundings. The notion that love and passion belong in the realm of creativity is well embodied in the beloved woman who is literally a work of art.

These meanings are available to the reader, although Darío's narrator does not present the story as any type of exemplary fable. The approach is light-spirited, emphasizing the amusing and surprising aspects of the story. The narrator makes sport of the hero for having the unlikely name of Recaredo, rhapsodizes over the charm of the heroine, and generally signals that the storytelling is a leisurely event to be enjoyed. The act of narrating itself seems to be taken less than seriously as the narrator playfully mocks his own casualness in providing data: "Did I tell you Recaredo was a sculptor? Well, in case I didn't say so, know it. He was a sculptor."

It is easy to see why stories of this type have helped to give Darío the reputation, in some quarters, as an irresponsibly frivolous writer. Particularly common is the assertion that, given the social problems of Latin America, a Nicaraguan writer could not truly afford to spend his talents creating such confectionary literary amusements. Darío was working with an organized literary esthetic, however, and sought certain specifiable ideals. The creation of a harmonious realm of art was meant to provide an alternative to the soiled, workaday reality that arose from technological progress. The celebration of erotic passion was to serve as a counterforce to the repressive influence of conservative Catholic-Hispanic culture.

The issue of how seriously to take Darío is unlikely to be resolved, given the dissimilar premises of many of his critics. Darío, today as in his lifetime, is most appreciated by authors and critics who generally favor a detached and abstract relationship between art and social realities; for example, the Mexican poet Octavio Paz has been one of the most eloquent and popular defenders of Darío. Those who believe literary writing to be, to some extent, a pragmatic form of communication concerning society and human nature tend to be repulsed by his refusal to convey "usable" meanings. Darío, who initially dismissed the issue, eventually became troubled over his penchant for decorative abstraction and began to write to comunicate more obvious meanings.

It should also be mentioned that Darío wrote many short fictions that were merely entertainments. A great believer in all manner of parapsychological and occult systems, he used material about supernatural happenings to construct stories recounting the transmigration of souls and the projection of astral auras. These popular stories, published in a vast number of newspapers and magazines, rely heavily on an "astounding" turn of plot and on an elaborate, if somewhat conventional, set of techniques for generating suspense and suspending disbelief.

While many modernists favored verse as the most pure and rhythmic of forms, Manuel Gutiérrez Nájera (Mexico, 1859–1895) was able to win a wide audience for innovative and stylish prose. Under the pen names El Duque Job and Puck, as well as his given name, he published numerous brief narrative and descriptive pieces. In many cases, his readership was primarily a general newspaper and magazine public, and this circumstance should probably be taken into account when considering his more maudlin stories.

Current-day readers may initially be alienated by Gutiérrez Nájera's highly conventional subjects. A sentimentalist, he tended to create young heroines whose lives were ebbing away from grief and consumption (or, alternatively, child protagonists in a similar situation). A second, more cynical mode produced fictional treatments of faithless wives and demimondaines. Gutiérrez Nájera also specialized in the description of religious observances with a rather saccharine idealization of various sacramental occasions.

If thematics were the sole basis for judging the man's work, any republication of his writings would be unjustifiable. But Gutiérrez Nájera was able to use these mass-appeal topics as a pretext for fashioning elegant, cosmopolitan prose. Within the conventional framework, individual elements of the narratives show a surprising degree of experimentation.

Gutiérrez Nájera was fascinated with the concept of stylishness and chic, and with finding fitting literary evocations of these hard-to-define qualities. Of course, all modernists were bound by their shared esthetic to be attentive to matters of literary style; many, like Rubén Darío, also were obsessed with human ornamentation in the forms of fashion and decor. Gutiérrez Nájera, however, seemed to gravitate to the larger question of what constituted fashion and how certain displays of objects and behavior could claim such privileged status.

"Después de las carreras" (After the Races), is an exemplar of this preoccupation. The plot concerns two young women: one is a wealthy belle who displays her finery at the races; the other a threadbare aristocrat forced to wait outside, and who suffers the conventional consumptive decline. The narrator closely observes the factors that make the races such a highly charged, almost magical event. The activity inside the elegant Hippodrome is not described, although it is at the heart of the story. Instead, the great social event is reflected obliquely through the rich heroine's excited primping for her appearance there, the poor woman's fleeting glimpses of the event and her later meditations. Many small details emphasize the significance given the racing meets, as, for example, the poor seamstress stationed at the periphery in case the ladies' finery should need repair or adjustment. The result is the semiveiled presentation of a complicated ritual capable of creating intense feelings of enchantment and excitement from both the included and the excluded protagonists.

The structure of the brief text and its cultural references augment its efforts to project cosmopolitan chic. As was fashionable among modernists, Gutiérrez Nájera dispensed with any substantial plot. Instead, there is a juxtaposition of scenes that highlight the effect of the central event and its attendant preparations. In this respect, it is worth nothing that the author could elaborate the same type of material with even less support from a narrative structure. "En el Hipódromo" (At the Hippodrome), a largely descriptive work included in the same collection as "Después de las carreras," makes the point. This nonfictional depiction of the fashionable racetrack would suggest that the author considered plot a comparatively dispensable item in his repertory of prose techniques.

The ideal of a cosmopolitan culture, seen as a break with the monolithic stagnation of Spanish-derived culture, also figures in other ways in "Después de las carreras:" Gutiérrez Nájera sprinkles French borrowings through his lexicon; similarly, he names his ill-fated heroine Manon, thereby establishing a bond with French literary culture as well as language. Besides this deference to French culture, he opens up his set of cultural references to include more exotic items; the wealthy young woman has a fur from Russia and clothing and luxury items from far-flung sources. In addition to esoteric and exotic allusions, the modernists embellished their work with extensive classic references, and in "Después de las carreras" a bust of Galatea is mentioned among the decorative inventory.

Even after noting these innovative features and appreciating the carefully designed rhythm patterns of the Spanish, it may be difficult for modern readers to find more than light entertainment in such prose. Gutiérrez Nájera is to some extent comparable to those Hollywood studio photographers who invested enormous talent and technical resources in the production of glamorous and magically voguish images. The author himself seems to be proclaiming the insubstantiality of his works by collecting them under the title *Cuentos frágiles* (1883; Fragile Stories); the posthumous *Cuentos color de humo* (1898; Smoke-Colored Stories) is titled in the same spirit.

At the same time, these stories should be seen as part of a larger plan to create a harmonious new art. The establishment of nonutilitarian prose, commonplace as it may seem now, was a true struggle in a literary culture that had not yet made space for artistic prose. The euphonious harmonies that Gutiérrez Nájera and others prized so highly were not merely ornamental, but one component of an overall project of striving toward beauty in an age of vulgarity and noisy commerce. These premises, which essentially made art into a quasi-religious exercise, were taken seriously enough to provide the impetus for a great deal of painstaking experimentation with prose style. The great emphasis on achieving a balanced and harmonious work was necessary as a corrective to the chaotic structure of previous prose efforts, whether this disorderly quality resulted from lack of interest in style or from romantic exaltation of wild disorder. Since then, writers have shifted their efforts to an attempt to prove that fiction need not exhibit perfect coherence to be considered art. Readers favoring innovative material have learned to distrust texts that seek to perpetuate the ideal of artistic harmony.

The modernist stories discussed thus far all belong to what is considered the "first modernism." This movement, including Martí, Gutiérrez Nájera, Darío, Julián del Casal (Cuba, 1863–1893), and José Asunción Silva (Colombia, 1865–1896), succeeded in wresting literary language from its realistic and romantic models and in revitalizing the rhythms of poetry and artistic prose. It ended with the deaths of all the major figures except Darío. The Nicaraguan poet still felt the need to share his developing esthetic ideas with a group of friends and colleagues. Although Darío formed alliances with a variety of writers, and moved about a great deal, he settled in Buenos Aires long enough to found a second modernist movement.

Writers associated with the later manifestations of modernism were less occupied with the basic groundbreaking effort of establishing a privileged status for artistic writing and a literary standard of language specifically designed to give esthetic pleasure. They were freer to pursue individual variations that eventually led directly away from the movement's original esthetic. Generally, their most innovative and impressive work was in verse. Ricardo Jaimes Freyre (Bolivia, 1868–1933) won renown with his 1899 *Castalia bárbara* (Barbarian Castalia), a modernistic accommodation of material from Norse mythology, but his short stories were not always indicative of his originality. Some prose works appear in the work of Amado Nervo (Mexico, 1870–1919), a poet with strong religious preoccupations whose work moves away from the artistic detachment and ironic distancing of much modernist writing. Among writers whose brief narrative reflected their most original artistic ideas, Manuel Díaz Rodríguez of Venezuela (1871–1927) merits special attention for his *Cuentos de color* (1899; Stories of Color). As the title suggests, these stories offer a virtual showcase of sensuously appealing artistic prose, seeking to provide literary correlatives for memorable real-world sensory perceptions. While other examples of unusual and noteworthy late-modernist prose could be cited, the real master of the form is Leopoldo Lugones (Argentina, 1874–1938). Co-leader with Darío of the modernist revival in Buenos Aires, Lugones was highly successful in working out new modernist versions of the traditional tale of supernatural terror.

Troubled and egomaniacal as well as skillful, Lugones was a habitual promoter of controversies. On the one hand, he worked to establish literature's right to stand free of immediate real-world concerns and to employ a language made for art, not for pragmatic communication. On the other hand, he was continually involving himself in literary and cultural projects laden with political implications. Throughout his career, Lugones's politics were on public display as they moved erratically to the right. He began with a utopian socialist-anarchist orientation, then cast that off as he fully entered the cultural establishment. He was placed in charge of the official cultural arm of the 1910 centennial celebrations, and composed patriotic verse. This establishment role does not seem to have assuaged his restlessness, and he began to experiment with extremely conservative, back-to-the-land notions of society. After his suicide, he was found to have been working on unmistakably fascist writings. These political attitudes, together with Lugones's irascibility in regard to many younger literary innovators, have given him something of a reputation as a sociocultural reactionary; but in literary language and structure, he was highly inventive.

Lugones's innovation may initially appear to consist of a collection of eccentric habits, and there is no doubt he was idiosyncratic in his work. He especially individualized his lexicon, incorporating an enormous variety of obscure and archaic terms. Jorge Luis Borges, to some extent a literary heir of Lugones, summarized this aspect of the older writer's work by saying, "Lugones believed a writer should use all the words in the dictionary."[4]

In writing short stories, Lugones favored unusual framing devices or overall structure that gave the appearance of nonfiction. He created fiction that would mimic the real-world document in the form of a testimony or deposition, personal diary, or lost fragment from a historical chronicle. His many inventive variants on the familiar fictional ploy of the found manuscript were useful in moving away from the by-now routine third-person narrator of so much nineteenth-century fiction, and the confessional first-person style that was its most common alternative. In addition, Lugones imaginatively obscured the circumstance that supposedly allowed the reader access to these pseudodocuments, thus adding an extra component of the unexplained to his tales of bizarre and esoteric happenings.

Erudition and the peculiar uses Lugones made of it also merit attention. He was extremely well informed about secret cults, exotic cultures, and little-known periods in Western history. Displaying accumulated cultural information in his stories, he avoided any attempt at exact historical re-creation. Instead, he preferred to mix genuine data with materials that were anachronistic to the story's time frame or even overtly spurious. This capricious intermixing of obscure fact and pseudofact is, of course, familiar to modern-day readers of Jorge Luis Borges.

"La estatua de sal" (The Pillar of Salt) from the 1919 collection *Los caballos de Abdera* (The Horses of Abdera) gives a good sampling of Lugones's creation of obscure and arcane ambience and literary summoning up of hidden cosmic forces, as well as of his narrative inventiveness. The nucleus of the story is an ancient oral legend about a supernaturally enlightened holy man from the days of the Desert Fathers. This legend is embedded in a multiple-narrative frame. The first narrator who appears merely hands over the narration to an individual known as the pilgrim; this person, after lengthy prefatory remarks, relates a story ascribed to one of the few surviving desert-dwelling ascetics. Even this monk is not the original source, however, for the legend has been transmitted through ages of oral retelling. This chain of storytellers not only sets up one of the unusual narrative inventions Lugones prized, but also puts one in mind of the mass of enigmas surrounding the early days of the Christian church, with its proliferation of competing accounts and mysterious variant sects.

The narrator designated as the pilgrim is clearly in awe of the monastic isolates and, in speaking of them, summons up the entire mystique surrounding the Desert Fathers. His description of the desolate, arid setting transforms it into a fantastic landscape where salt and sand scourge away the vegetation, where the times of the day "mingle into a single sadness," and the only visitors are "those who must expiate great crimes."

This pilgrim-narrator reveals himself to be a great believer in miraculous and supernatural occurrences. His fervent belief makes him an ideal voice for conveying the magical qualities of a time in which Christianity was still a strange and deviant cult peopled with zealots, ascetics, prophets, visionaries, and wonder-workers. The pilgrim insists that the hermits' extreme sacrifices and penances, including daily self-inflicted wounds, "prevented many plagues, wars and earthquakes. . . ; the sacrifices and prayers of the just are the keys to the roof of the universe."

Only after this elaborate evocation of a magical era does the actual story, a fairly meager narrative, begin. The monk Sosistrato, who over the years has become "almost transparent" with age and holiness, receives from a mysterious visitor an invitation to visit the ruined cities of the plain and free Lot's wife from her transformation into a pillar of salt. The holy man carries out this plan, but cannot resist demanding what the revived woman's last sight had been. The answer, undivulged to the reader, strikes the pure monk dead.

The story exemplifies an aspect of modernism Lugones especially favored: the suggestion, by literary means, of terrible cosmic forces capable of wreaking great changes in the life of a man. It is only one of many narratives in which an individual, through curiosity, or simply unwittingly, establishes a connection with these "strange forces"—to use the title of Lugones's 1906 collection of short fiction (*Las fuerzas extrañas*). Among the bizarre plots that support these stories are the cultivation of "the flower of death" (Viola Acheronita), the discovery of distressing secrets about the evolution of men and simians ("Yzur"), and various scientific and theosophical inquiries resulting in the re-searcher's destruction.

These stories may to some degree seem to be idle thrillers, distin-guished from pulp fiction only by their elaborately imaginative de-velopment. It is true that some of the models for this type of amazing tale were Edgar Allan Poe and the later, deranged, Guy de Maupassant. It should be noted, however, that Poe and other masters of horror, usually relegated to a secondary rank in the United States, were consistently taken more seriously in Europe and Latin America. While Americans tend to see only the horror-producing mechanisms, many European and Latin American readers looked to these authors as providing channels to alternate realms of experience. There was a fashionable belief that the best horror stories could bring the reader insights into the hidden, terrifying interconnections of all phenomena. This belief was so strong that it manifested itself in occult practices and theosophical meditations as well as in the writing of short stories. Virtually all those associated with late modernism had some involvement with occult research and inquiry. This aspect of their activity was the nonliterary manifestation of the same desire to penetrate universal mysteries that underlies Lugones's more bizarre tales.

While stressing the esoteric thought of modernism, one should not overlook the playful and ironic elements in Lugones's presentation. The principal distancing factor in "La Estatua de Sal" is the attitude of the pilgrim. This narrator is more of a true believer than any educated modern reader could conceivably be. He fervently insists that the devil flung himself down in howling despair at the feet of the holy monks and that the monk Sosistrato was sustained by doves that fed him seeds. Presenting as fact these typical embellishments of oral legend, the pilgrim sets a distance between himself and the reader. This gap is skillfully exploited at the story's end. The monk's death has its potentially ludicrous side, since simple gossipy human curiosity has been the trivial cause of his downfall. The pilgrim, though, takes the event with the greatest seriousness, requesting all who hear the tale to pray for the monk's soul. Handled in this way, the ending provides both an occasion for awe and an irony. Such duplicity—combining the "put-on" with a respect for the cosmic mysteries—is central to Lugones's highly ambiguous magical stories.

The above remarks suggest the scope of Lugones's most famous brief-narrative strategies, but do not exhaust what this inventive writer did within the genre. At moments when a feeling for the land and the traditional past had claimed the imagination of many, Lugones produced rural stories, often lyrical and elegaic in their portrayal of the vanished epoch of the gaucho. These beautifully idealized images of the past are part of Lugones's notion of returning to a historical time in which urbanization, bureaucratization, and the cultural fragmentation of the gaucho had not yet produced their effects. Like the occult stories, these romantic tales are skillfully constructed with many elegant eccentricities of vocabulary and narrative device.

In effect, any generalization about Lugones's orientation must be qualified, for he was continually revising his esthetic program. It is this willingness to rethink his ideals and practices that makes him an important link between modernism and the subsequent literary movements of the 1920s, variously known as expressionism, vanguardism, or by the names of specific experimental groups. One can say that by the beginning of the vangard era, Lugones had moved out of the modernist esthetic and was concentrating on new elaborations of a highly figurative language.

This movement away from modernism and his renewed interest in metaphor made him in many ways similar to the youthful vanguardistas, however, his relations with the newer writers were decidedly troubled. The older man's crotchety pronouncements on literature made him an object of fun, particularly as the younger writers sought visible figures against whom to rebel. Only some years after this tumultuous period did Jorge Luis Borges retrospectively proclaim Lugones one of the great initiators of the 1920s revolution.

Despite his difficulties with younger writers, Lugones was important in advancing the career of the next great innovator of the Latin American short story, Horacio Quiroga (1878–1937) of Uruguay. Hearing of a modernist who was submersed in depression after the accidental murder of a friend, Lugones felt a stirring of his interest in the unusual. He sought out Quiroga and sponsored him on an expedition to the wilder far reaches of northern Argentina. The effects of these literary-historical events belong, however, to the next period in the development of the Latin American short story.

                                                            Naomi Lindstrom
University of Texas, Austin

THE SPANISH AMERICAN
SHORT STORY FROM
QUIROGA TO BORGES

John S. Brushwood

Quiroga and the Basis of the
Twentieth-Century Short Story

If asked for the name of an outstanding Spanish American *cuentisa* ("short-story writer"), a specialist in the literature would very likely think of Horacio Quiroga (Uruguay, 1878–1937) or Jorge Luis Borges (Argentina, 1899–). A second probability is corollary—that two decades ago, the answer would have been Quiroga; more recently, Borges would come to mind first. The latter's substantial influence goes back farther than two decades to the mid-1940s, however, some years passed before his name became virtually a household word internationally. This chapter does not undertake an analysis of the complete Borges phenomenon, but considers some of his early stories. From Quiroga's first important collection, *Cuentos de amor, de locura y de muerte* (Stories of Love, Madness and Death) in 1917 to Borges's *Ficciones* in 1944, the trajectory of short fiction shows a gradual but clear change in subject matter and in narrative technique.

Quiroga was the first Spanish American writer to pay close attention to how a story is made, and at the same time, dedicate himself almost exclusively to writing short fiction. In a statement of principles for the *cuentista*, he sets forth several ideas that are especially interesting because of his importance as *magister*.[1] Although Quiroga did not consistently assume such a role for himself and was quite aware that some younger writers were not entirely sympathetic to his work, his decalogue for the perfect *cuentista* states his case in no uncertain terms. He first exhorts the writer to have limitless faith in his literary master, and specifically mentions Poe, Maupassant, Kipling, and Chekov. The first two are quite clearly present in Quiroga's work; Kipling is apparent in the stories about anthropomorphized jungle beasts; Chekov's presence is not as easy to specify, but there is certainly no reason to doubt its existence. Beyond this oath of allegiance, Quiroga says that the writer should know before beginning the narration how the story is going to develop. It seems unlikely that he would have much patience with the writer whose characters take charge of the work. He warns against excessive use of adjectives, claiming that if the writer controls language well enough to choose the best substantive, modifiers need be used only sparingly. Writing under the impulse of emotion should be avoided, Quiroga says; once the emotion has cooled, however, the writer does well to re-create it in the experience of his work. Interesting an audience should not be a concern; rather, the *cuentista* should feel certain that what he writes is of interest to the characters about whom he is writing.

In general, these principles suggest a rather comfortable fit into the realist-naturalist tradition. That is indeed where Quiroga is based in literary history, but with modifications caused by the Spanish American literary milieu. He began writing in the early years of the twentieth century, toward the end of *modernismo* and at a time when realism and naturalism were generally recognized, but not always understood. One of his early stories, "Cuento sin razó, pero cansado" (1901; Story Without Cause, But Weary), may be safely thought of as *modernista* because one of its qualities is the sense of ennui associated with the French decadents. There is also in it some of naturalism's inevitability, and this characteristic becomes dominant in many stories, including the well-known "La gallina degollada" (1909; "The Decapitated Chicken").[2]

In this story, four idiot brothers commit an act of violence that is suggested to them by their having witnessed an ordinary act that seems analogous—to them—and quite acceptable. Quiroga introduces the brothers in an initial scene, then provides some background followed by emphasis on the parents' marital problems. The conflict that is developed in much of the story is based on the attitude of the parents toward their offspring. When this conflict reaches a climax, it points the reader in a direction different from that actually taken by the story. The narrator—always completely in control of the characters and recounting their actions without detailed characterization—removes the brothers from their regular routine, relates how they witnessed the stimulus action, and returns them to the place in which he first described them. Their subsequent action, wordless and in common accord, is an inevitable result of their mental condition.

The action of "La gallina degollada" takes place in the environs of Buenos Aires, but the story is in no way regionalistic. Quiroga often placed his stories in settings that were familiar to him, but his themes are universal. In "Juan Darién" (1920), the jungle is a factor, but not in terms of the man-against-nature theme found in many works located in unsettled areas. Rather, "Juan Darién" is a story of human injustice in the most general sense, not in terms of an attack on a specific or localized social problem. An animal is transformed into a human being and when his identity is discovered, he suffers the fate of those who threaten society because they are different.

The general structure of "Juan Darién" is what one would expect in a realist story: introduction, exposition of conflict, development, climax, and denouement. It is not a realistic story; it is a fantasy, and Quiroga never leaves any room for doubt about what kind of tale we are reading. At the beginning, the narrator states the fact of the animal's marvelous transformation. There is no time to wonder whether or not there may be some natural explanation for this phenomenon. We are dealing with a kind of fairy tale, and the language so indicates when the narrator uses expressions that are similar to English. "Once there was . . ." or "Well, of course. . . ," as introductions to paragraphs. The conflict in "Juan Darién" is between animal violence and human violence. Humans are always unjust; their only redeeming trait appears to be in the maternal role—the mother alone knows "the sacred rights of life."

Violence is frequent in Quiroga's work, but its signficance varies in important ways. In "La gallina degollada," it creates horror; in "Juan Darién," it is related to justice and injustice. In "El hombre muerto" (1920; "The Dead Man"), the protagonist comes to a violent end by accident, and one thinks less about the violence itself than about the man's awareness, or lack of awareness, of his condition. The general ambience of "el hombre muerto" tends to make the story appear more regionalistic than is actually the case. The setting is tropical and rural. The man falls on his machete in the course of his work and dies in a period of thirty minutes that are accounted for in the narration. There is no surprise ending, nothing that need be withheld in a discussion of how it works out. It is impossible to summarize the story without duplicating it, however, because the experience of this narrative is the man's growing awareness of his condition. The basic conflict is quite simply between life and death; its development is what the man thinks of his total situation (his immediate condition and its implications). Quiroga uses repetition with good effect as his protagonist becomes increasingly aware of what is happening to him and what it means in terms of the world in which he has lived. The narrator speaks mainly in free, indirect style, so we see what the man sees even though we are being informed by the third-person voice; an occasional comment from this point of view does not alter the basic narration in any significant way. Probably the outstanding device used by Quiroga in this story is a shift of focus in the last paragraph so that we are no longer seeing as the man sees but as he is seen. This change justifies the title; before this conclusion, the man is dying, but has not reached the end. The fact that "El hombre muerto" cannot be synopsized satisfactorily characterizes it as a more modern story than the other two by Quiroga. It would be difficult, and pointless, to say that one manner is more typical of the author than the other.

The perspective in which we see Quiroga in the early twentieth century as a kind of pillar of the Spanish American short story may be illuminated by reference to two stories by authors of the same genera- tion. One of these, "En provincia" (1914; In the Provinces) is by Augusto D'Halmar [Augusto Geomine Thompson] (Chile, 1882–1950), who is considered a naturalist writer; the other is "El hombre que parecía un caballo" (1915; "The Man Who Resembled a Horse"), by Rafael Arévalo Martínez (Guatemala, 1884–   ), who may be called either modernist or postmodernist. Neither of these stories is typical of either naturalism or modernism; each, however, has sufficient charac- teristics of the heritage that was Quiroga's, that their publication, so contemporaneous to Quiroga's own stories, emphasizes the sense of change that one experiences in reading the latter's work.

The small-town atmosphere of D'Halmar's story is faithful to the title, but identification with a specific geographical area is extremely dif- ficult. The protagonist, an unimportant employee of a commercial firm, is a confirmed bachelor whose only social contact is made through playing a musical instrument. The humdrum quality of his life and, indeed, the generally slow pace of the town are readily appreciable; however, the effect of the story is not to elicit sympathy for a lonely person—he is quite content with his life. The conflict is triggered by a woman who involves him in an adulterous affair, using him for her own benefit. "En provincia" will not do as a textbook example of naturalism, because the case of adultery is so extreme as to seem used as satire and because the situation is not treated as though it were a clinical study. It is narrative procedure that gives the story its special personality.

The protagonist is the first-person narrator. He introduces himself, describes his situation and the way he lives, and gives a few words about his background. Then he comments on his ambivalence concerning whether or not to tell his story, and concludes that although he will write it, no one will ever see it. Now the reader enters into a fascinating relationship with the narrator—the secret is out, or is going to be. It is worth noting that D'Halmar does not use the familiar device of the "found" manuscript. Of course, if we are to believe the narrator, someone must have found what he wrote, and he did not intend to have it discovered. The important effect is that the narrator's attitude toward the telling is really a part of the story we read, and the first conflict we are aware of has to do with that attitude. Then the protagonist moves into an account of the most important event in his life. This second conflict develops on the basis of his natural rights as an individual against the exigencies of social organization. Repeated episodes of sustained emotional intensity bring this conflict to a climax. The man's acceptance of his role, at this point, completes his characterization of himself and brings the reader to the starting point of the story of the adultery.

Arévalo Martínez's "El hombre que parecía un caballo" is more character sketch than traditionally plotted story. The narrative does move in time, enough to indicate change taking place in a friendship, but even this process of change is essentially a means of characterizing Aretal, the principal figure. A metaphor is established in terms of the equine analogy, which begins with reference to physical appearance and then becomes relevant to the more subtle manifestations of Aretal's personality. Arévalo Martínez also uses many metaphors that are very *modernista,* such as references to jewels, and the word azure to indicate the soul or the finer side of human personality. The story has its amusing side, created especially by Aretal's exterior similarity to a horse. He holds his head to one side, trots around the salon, sidles up to ladies, and whinnies. The revelation of his character is far more profound than these examples might indicate, however, and since we see him entirely from the narrator's point of view, the story is actually an evaluation of Aretal's personality.

Arévalo Martínez's affinity for *modernismo* is apparent enough in "El hombre que parecía un caballo," but he avoids the lush estheticism that characterized some *modernista* work and provoked a movement by some writers toward portrayal of the commonplace, the familiar. This is the phenomenon frequently called *criollismo*.[3] In the early years of the century, there was a complex of "isms" that were different from each other in some respects but not in others, and were also concurrent to a degree. One of the functions of *modernismo* was as a reaction against the ugliness of realism and naturalism, and criollismo was a reaction aganst the hyperestheticism of the *modernistas,* but these movements and countermovements did not cancel the characteristics of any of the forces involved. No movement comes to a standstill when a reaction makes itself felt. That is why "En provincia" and "El hombre que parecía un caballo" show characteristics of two different movements without being perfect examples. Change is taking place; at the same time, some stories continue to hew close to the line of one "ism" or another.

Alfonso Hernández Catá's (Cuba, 1885–1940) "Noventa días" (Ninety Days) is a naturalist story about a deteriorating infatuation told as if it were a case history. Its development follows a very orthodox pattern in which the narrator establishes the setting, introduces the principal character, and then initiates the action, which in turn follows a standard pattern. Spring, an important factor in the atmosphere, becomes even more important in the action as the narrator personifies the season and shows how it inspires an infatuation that is doomed never to blossom into real love. The conflict is represented in the personalities of the two principals, who are entirely different from each other and little inclined to make concessions once the magic of spring is lost; it is developed through a series of similar incidents until the story ends in tragedy. Hernández Catá's story, on the trajectory of literary history, could fit comfortably before or after *modernismo.*

These early stories use a wide variety of anecdotal material, the nature of which says a great deal about what the authors were doing in ways that went beyond classification by literary movement. Of the three Quiroga stories, "La gallina degollada" may seem at first to be terrifyingly real. It is certainly terrifying, but on second thought it seems less a representation of reality than "El hombre muerto," because in the first story Quiroga's material is a psychological principle rather than a normally observed happening. "Juan Darién" is a fantasy that may have been born of observed reality, but its incident comes no closer to experienced reality than allegory does. On the basis of "La gallina degollada" and "Juan Darién," one would hardly call Quiroga a *criollista,* since these stories are not reproductions of everyday, familiar

Spanish American reality. "El hombre muerto" is a different matter. Its theme is universal, but the actual happening takes place in the tropics where a man has a banana grove and works with a machete. These facts provide some of the quality of our-own-Spanish-American-reality sought by the *criollistas*.

In fact, the themes of all the stories mentioned so far are universal, although some of the material may be slightly less so. "El hombre muerto" uses the most clearly regionalistic material. The setting of "En provincia" is provincial, but not identified with a region in that the action itself is not influenced by regional characteristics; "Noventa días" belongs anyplace where spring suggests romance. In both stories, the authors are relating ordinary human situations, but it is doubtful that there is a sense of closeness, of personal relationship, between them and the material. Interestingly, the story that may seem most fanciful, "El hombre que parecía un caballo," is probably closest to real life, a fantasized account of something that really happened.

Narrative technique has a great deal to do with how the reader understands the story. Arévalo Martínez might have told of his friendship with Señor Aretal in countless different ways. His decision to use the horse analogy in combination with words suggesting great refinement creates a contrast that is both amusing and perceptive. If he had narrated a typically realist story, the actions of the two people with respect to each other would be the same, but the effect would be different. The story could be more psychological, for example, but the suggestive contrast would not be emphasized. In the case of "La gallina degollada," Quiroga decided to characterize the parents more than the idiot sons. This creates a more complex understanding of the parents while presenting the four boys with clinical objectivity; as their role becomes preeminent, attention focuses on the psychological principle. The same story told any other way might change emphasis, but not the relationship of persons to actions. Quiroga might even have chosen to stress the ambience of a particular area, in which case the story would have seemed more *criollista*, as does "Juan Darién."

Innovative Narration in the Late 1920s and Early 1930s

Narrative strategies in the early twentieth century are more sophisticated than they are usually thought to be. It is hardly surprising that the most obvious techniques are related to point of view. In addition, the

authors' interpretation of story material is effected in many other ways
that control emphasis. This concern for narrative strategy is characteristic of the realist novelists. It should be clear, regarding this point, that
realism does not equate with *criollismo*. The latter refers to theme, not
to techniques of narrating. And with regard to *criollista* themes, one
should notice that what a writer in Quito sees as charming local color
may be quite different from what creates the same reaction in a *cuentista* who lives in Buenos Aires.

In the 1920s and the early 1930s, we find a certain tension between
folklore and sophistication in Spanish American fiction. The folkloric
stories of Miguel Angel Asturias (Guatemala, 1899–1974) are quite
different from the sophisticated, urban stories of Eduardo Mallea (Argentina, 1903–   ). Since folklore generally suggests country folk, the
folklore-versus-sophistication contrast becomes rural-versus-urban.
However, neither of these two polarities describes the tension satisfactorily. Still another variation exists wholly within the urban setting—
between, for example, the cosmopolitanism of Mallea and the middle-
class heterodoxy (glorification of the common man) of Roberto Arlt
(Argentina, 1900–1942). It is important to insist on the word "tension"
rather than "conflict," because the lines are not clearly drawn: Asturias
deals with folklore in a highly sophisticated way; Demetrio Aguilera-
Malta (Ecuador, 1909–1981) deals with rural folk in a stylized fashion;
Manuel Rojas (Chile, 1896–1973) uses material that verges on the
folkloric, but in an urban situation. The term most frequently used with
reference to this period is vanguardism, to point out its innovative
characteristic; however, others might prefer calling it a period of vanguardism and *costumbrismo*. One finds in almost all the *cuentistas*,
regardless of their story material, a tendency to write in a different way,
to find the technique that best suits the material.

Eduardo Mallea's first published volume was *Cuentos para una inglesa desesperada*, (1926; Stories for an English Lady in Distress). These
stories, although they are never likely to be considered great works, are
of considerable importance in the evolution of the genre in Spanish
America. The author appears to be looking for something new. There are
suggestions of decadence and even of an earlier type of *modernismo* in
these first stories, which are completely different from his later work. He
seems to be pulling away from a tradition, appealing to the symbols of
modernity (automobiles, Yale banners, music of the 1920s), suggesting
the jazz age in a nearly flippant tone that wishes, at the same time, to
announce its own basic seriousness. Here Mallea experiments with

language much more than in his better-known works. He uses anaphora to suggest boredom, synonyms to move toward variety; sentences without finite verbs set the scene; other sentences consisting of single words create an impressionistic effect. Unmodified substantives work together to create atmosphere. There is a feeling of worldliness in this book, and reader identification with a narrator who, alternating voices between first and third person, seems to be searching for a way to capture the change that he senses in a large city.

The concept of short fiction was obviously changing; many younger writers preferred intimate study of character reaction rather than outside observation of events. This tendency is especially apparent in the prose of writers associated with the Mexican magazine *Contemporáneos* (which flourished between the years of 1928–1931) and other writers of the same age. There were also writers in other countries who were changing the idea of the short story in the same way—Enrique Labrador Ruiz (Cuba, 1902–   ) or Silvina Ocampo (Argentina, 1906–   )

Efrén Hernańdez's (Mexico, 1903–1958) "Tachas" (1928; Cross-outs) builds on the contrast between the reality of a classroom and that of the wandering mind (no less real, of course) of a boy who is inclined to think of anything but the matter at hand. The story opens with an exact statement of the time of day; this information is the only part of the story that is truly precise. Next is a question by the teacher, "What are *tachas*?" (The translation of this word becomes a problem; it has several meanings in Spanish, and there is no English word with the same range of use.) The first-person narrator, who sees only from his own point of view, confesses that he has not prepared the lesson and is not even paying attention. He is interested in other things, from passing clouds to street noises. Periodically, the teacher's question brings him back to the physical classroom reality, but he is soon lost again in contemplation. The narrator relates specific events in past tense, but adopts the present tense when he speaks of matters that last longer than the classroom scene. One section, for example, becomes epistemologic when the teacher's question makes him wonder if it is possible to know what *tachas* means, if it is possible to know anything.

Thanks to the device of juxtaposing past and present tenses to signify external and internal actions, the reader realizes that the story's several pages correspond to a moment in time, just as telling a dream takes more time than the dream itself. Finally, the teacher directs his question to the narrator, who undertakes to answer in an exaggeratedly pedantic fashion that is quite inappropriate to the character we have come to know through his mental rovings. Hernández is fond of the humor created by such a contrast, and handles it very adroitly. The conflict between classroom reality and the boy's interests produces warmth as well, but it is a metaphor of a deeper conflict, that is, between the natural and the absurd, which, climactically, the boy relates to his own personality.

Agustín Yáñez's (Mexico, 1904–1980) "Baralipton" (1930) resembles "Tachas" in that the narration again plays on the conflict between the reality external to the chracter and his wandering mind. In the Yáñez story, the protagonist is preparing for his final examination as a medical student, and at the same time is taking account of his situation, trying to make reality seem truly real. The narrative comes very close to free association, but there is some comment by a third-person narrator other than the protagonist. In "Baralipton," as in "Tachas," there are indications of an author who is sharply aware of the fact that he is making a fiction and who comments on the process within the story itself. The most interesting incident of this kind in "Tachas" is a passage in which the narrative voice discusses the question of to whom the words are addressed, and this self-conscious alienation is of great importance in characterization. In "Baralipton," the protagonist is given form during the course of narration. The story begins with a sound and a date, and then a reference to a circumstance. Within this circumstance, the narrator begins a sentence with "But he—here protagonist—was preparing university examinations . . ." Following this sentence, the narrator refers only to "protagonist" (with no preceding article) until the second section of the story, entitled "Second State." In this part, protagonist acquires a more specific identity and may be Pedro, Juan, or Francisco. The narrator, still in the process of designing the story, suggests that "we" opt for Juan and then simplify that to J.

In subsequent pages of mental wanderings, Yáñez employs several techniques that reinforce the feeling of disorganization. The structure itself surprises the reader because the divisions do not seem logical in terms of titles or of length. For example, there is a "Second Part of the Third Part," which carries its own subtitle of "First Psalm and Chapter," and this is followed by a "Last Part" containing subsections called "Final Meditation" and "Final Scene." In prose style, he makes substantive associations, that is, without finite verbs (a strategy he often uses) and some plays on words and on sounds. These techniques create effects contrary to those of rational discourse and intensify the question of identity that is inherent in wondering whether J, having become a physician, is different from the J of thirty minutes earlier, before he had been granted the title.

The material of "Tachas" and of "Baralipton" is ordinary life. The extent to which the stories may or may not be autobiographical has nothing to do with their reality because the material with which they deal is just as familiar to the author as that of any realist novel. The narratives are not realist in the literary use of the term, however, because the narrative strategies are different. Nevertheless, one can certainly say that the experience of these stories is eminently realistic.

Jaime Torres Bodet's (Mexico, 1902–1974) "Nacimiento de Venus" (1931; Venus Rising From the Sea) is a rather different kind of story because it depends on the combination of a modern event and a classic allusion. The event is the shipwreck of a girl named Lidia, and the first part of the story is a kind of maritime debate concerning whether she will be washed ashore in Italy or in Greece. This narrative is highly poetic, and its fundamental pleasure is in the suggestive quality of each sentence. It is as if a statue were afloat, and the conflict established is between art and life. There is a flashback to the shipwreck and to Lidia's everyday reality; then the narrative returns to the figure on the beach and the allusion to Botticelli's painting. Any move Lidia makes creates a new work of art. This story, as much a prose poem as it is a narrative, again emphasizes the creative function metaphorically insofar as literature is concerned. The material in this case is more than an incident; it is an awareness of art and of myth.

During this period of innovative fiction (late 1920s and early 1930s), some stories dealt with subjects that are more typically (or more exotically) Spanish American, and many are notable for their highly imaginative treatment of indigenous folklore. In Leyendas de Guatemala (1930; Legends of Guatemala), Miguel Angel Asturias embellishes stories from Maya tradition by adding his own imagery.

Asturias's relationship to his material is unusual. He was away from his native country, living in Paris, when he met and studied with a famous anthropologist who was investigating Mayan culture. Asturias experienced a sense of familiarity with this tradition, and understood that he was now discovering more fully some of his own heritage. He appropriated the legends for use as story material, and added much of himself to their telling.

"La leyenda de la Tatuana" (1930; "The Legend of the Tattooed Woman") is the story of a slave girl who has the ability to make herself invisible. She was granted this power by a magus figure so she might be saved from execution. The story does not explicate Mayan legend, but in the act of telling it the narrator interrupts to say "the legend continues," indicating that the narrator thinks of himself as an intermediary rather than as an author. This has the effect of removing the reader from the existential significance of the ancient myth. The narrator adds a special quality to the story by repetition and by using colors with a generosity that makes one think of the embroidery on a Mayan *huipil*.

The *Leyendas de Guatemala*, both folkloric and regionalistic, are not vehicles of social protest, although Asturias's later work became strongly denunciatory. In fact, throughout Spanish America the mix of regionalism and social protest is variable, in short stories by writers known primarily for their novels, such as Ricardo Güiraldes (Argentina, 1886–1927) and Rómulo Gallegos (Venezuela, 1884–1969), and even among the strongly committed writers of the Ecuadorean *grupo de Guayaquil*. The volume most freqently identified with the latter group is *Los que se van* (1930; Those Who Are Departing), which is made up of stories by Demetrio Aguilera-Malta, Enrique Gil Gilbert (Ecuador, 1912–   ), and Joaquín Gallegos Lara (Ecuador, 1911–1947). These three young writers differed from each other in many ways, but they shared a deep sympathy for the humble people of Ecuador, and their stories capture essential qualities of the people's culture. Their lives appear closer to natural elements; violence is always present, more so in the works of Gil Gilbert and Gallegos Lara than in those of Aguilera-Malta, though in the stories of Aguilera-Malta violence always threatens even when it is not overt. In the works of the first two, the narrator controls the situation absolutely, and the reader becomes involved because of the horror he is called on to witness. Aguilera-Malta involves the reader more subtly.

His "El cholo que se vengó" (1930; The *Cholo*'s Vengeance) is a very short story in which violence is understood but not exercised. The vengeance of the *cholo*, a geographical-racial native of Ecuador, is of a very special kind and its nature is the basis of the story. The narrator does nothing to indicate that this kind of vengeance is typical; however, he suggests very strongly that violent emotions are characteristic of the people. The story is a monologue by the *cholo* in which he addresses the woman who rejected him in favor of another suitor. The monologue is intercalated with narrator's reference to the sea by which the couple is sitting. The protagonist's spoken words are simple, although the feeling behind them is complex, with the sea itself communicating the depth and intensity of his emotions. The overall effect of "El cholo que se vengó" is not protest, but deep appreciation of the emotions of apparently simple people.

There is a kind of regionalism even in Manuel Rojas's "El vaso de leche" (1929; "The Glass of Milk") in that it involves a port and a young seaman who wishes to establish his independence. Such a large part of Chile is seacoast that subject matter of this kind appears frequently in the country's literature. The theme of the story, however, is utterly universal. Stripped to its narrative bones, it tells of a young man who desperately needs help and at last finds it in the person of a mother figure. "El vaso de leche" has the typical structure of a realist story: circumstance, introduction of character, and development of plot that unfolds on the basis of a conflict expressed in ways that are metaphors or near metaphors of each other.

The conflict may be described as one between hunger and pride. Although he is hungry, the young man enjoys freedom that contrasts with earlier restrictions. At the same time, both hunger and freedom are associated with the sea, which functions in opposition to the city. The protagonist may gain relief from two sources: an English sailor in the port and a woman who runs a lunch room in the city. Food is offered by the sailor in such a way that the protagonist's pride does not allow him to accept it. The glass of milk, however, is offered by someone identified with the city and with a restricted life. There are several interrelationships among these contrasts that make the story especially rich.

Regionalism Predominant: The Mid-1930s

While both cosmopolitanism and criollismo existed during the 1920s and early 1930s, the former tended to predominate; however, as the decade moved on, criollismo became more important. The shift in relative importance does not indicate that criollismo had become a clearly defined genre. Among stories that make use of peculiarly American referents, narrative strategies vary significantly, as do authors' comprehensive notions of how a story is made. "La botija" (1933; "Buried Treasure") by Salvador Salazar Arrué (known as Salarrué) (El Salvador, 1899–1975) and "La plaza de las carretas" (1937; Oxcart Stop) by Enrique Amorim (Uruguay, 1900–1960) are at opposite ends of a continuum so far as plot is concerned. "La botija" depends entirely on a tricky story, while the few events in "La plaza de las carretas" hardly make a story at all, the narrative instead being replete with atmosphere.

At different points along the continuum, many stories focus on different problems of social justice with varying degrees of artistic success.

"La botija" is the story of a farmer who is obsessed by the possibility of finding hidden treasure. In pursuit of this dream, he accumulates a modest fortune that he buries so no one will be able to say that there is no buried treasure in the area. Salarrué uses the speech of country people, a technique that lets him present the story from their point of view; a problem arises, however, because he does not maintain this focus consistently, and therefore the tone becomes patronizing. None of this affects the value of the story as a cleverly worked anecdote. It means that plot dominates characterization and tone.

"La plaza de las carretas" is more markedly regionalistic. The title refers to a method of transporting freight in Uruguay—a caravan of oxcarts—and the plaza, the overnight stopping place. Amorim's narrator uses first person to establish himself as knowledgeable with respect to the material, but he does not play a role of importance. Although we know that we are seeing the situation from his point of view, the general effect of the narrative is that of third-person voice. Indeed, the story might have been more credible if the first-person device had not been used, because the language is not what we are likely to expect of people who know a lot about oxcarts. Images abound; poetic suggestion is a basic strategy, as evidenced in an English approximation of the first sentence: "It came out of the distance, altering the rigorous discipline of night, grinding the silence on its bone-dry axles."

One could argue that the style is too poetic for the subject matter, but in spite of that, Amorim manages to create a satisfying impression of the overnight stop. He does so by using language to enrich the circumstance rather than match it. The resulting effect is similar to that achieved by Asturias in *Leyendas de Guatemala*. Very little happens in "La plaza de las carretas" that suggests a plot line, although the description of the situation is full of interesting detail. The thirst of the oxen on arrival is one of the important components of the total impression, as one of the animals dies after drinking too much water. A number of different people are mentioned, but not fully characterized. One young woman's presence suggests the possibility of a plot, but the story does not develop. Amorim does not indulge in extensive backgrounds. He sticks mainly with the scene itself, the segment of time that corresponds to the brief night's stop. The people are parts of that scene, but neither characterization nor action is as important as atmosphere. The event, as far as it is developed, communicates a feeling of authenticity.

Rural life in Uruguay is portrayed in the fiction of this time as a tough, minimal, generally unattractive existence. One of the most prolific *cuentistas* in Spanish America, Juan José Morosoli (Uruguay, 1899–1957) published several volumes of stories about life in the country or in provincial towns. His work underscores the dreariness of life as portrayed in "La plaza de las carretas." Compared with Amorim, Morosoli is less poetic, more inclined to characterize; however, his stories tend to have very little action—a natural condition in the kind of life he describes.

Complaints about the quality of life occur frequently in many of these stories. Even in narratives based on a specific problem, the more general condition would presumably continue even if the smaller one were resolved. Francisco Rojas González's (Mexico, 1905–1951) "Trigo de invierno" (1937; Winter Wheat) is about a rural Mexican Jean Valjean, that is, it centers on an excessive punishment for a minor theft. The story told by the man's wife arouses indignation about a personal injustice, but the larger problems as it relates to the society is amply apparent.

Rojas González is probably best known for his stories of rural life, and especially among the *indígenas*. He dealt with social problems in the city also, and one of his later stories, "Una cáscara en la banqueta" (1945; An Orange Peel on the Sidewalk), is especially interesting for its techniques. An unnamed man, starving, is in Alameda Park in Mexico City. Rojas González presents him as a person whose fundamental dignity is corroded by his economic condition and, consequently, by his physical desperation. The reader's awareness of his state is effected not by reference to background, but by means of a few adjectives and actions, for example, as he adjusts the knot of his worn-out tie. In very concise narration, Rojas González describes the man's immediate surroundings—the person who passes by eating an orange and drops the peel on the sidewalk, another who almost steps on the peel, the restaurant sign that the man sees in hallucinatory fashion, a mother and child who pass by and think he is drunk. The narrator stays rigorously focused on the scene; there is absolutely no background. We never learn the man's name; we have no idea how or why he has reached the sorry state in which we see him. "Una cáscara en la banqueta" is a carefully preserved slice of reality that can be related to a larger circumstance in any way the reader may choose.

Among the *cuentistas* who have written about the Indian in Spanish America, José María Arguedas (Peru, 1911–1969) is especially noted for combining social protest with a deep sensitivity for the Indians' view of reality. He was also sharply aware of his own biracial background, culturally as well as physically. One of the principal techniques he uses is making inanimate objects come alive. In "Warma Kukay" (1935; "Puppy Love") ". . . the whiteness of the wall seemed to move, like clouds chasing along the slopes of Chawala."

In the story, a boy, the narrator, contrasts himself with the Indian Kutu, feels himself to be an outsider, especially because he is in love with an Indian girl much older than he. There are two conflicts in his life. One is in regard to his belonging to two cultures, with the consequent feeling of being outside; the second is between the indignation and impotence he feels at having to confront an injustice by the landowner with respect to the girl. The situation is a standard one in Spanish American fiction— white landowner takes an attractive native woman into the house as a servant-mistress. Arguedas adds freshness by making his boy-narrator the offended male (Kutu is the offended male in the realm of adult love) and developing the story on the basis of the two struggles that criss-cross in action and significance. The boy is not really within the Indian culture, a condition that is exacerbated as far as his love is concerned by the fact that he is only a child. At the same time, the white landowner becomes the ultimate villain.

There is a considerable protest concerning the Indian's—or peasant's—role as a tool of the military, in Augusto Céspedes's (Bolivia, 1904–   ) "El pozo" (1936; "The Well"), but the deeper meaning of the story is the senselessness of the Chaco War. This war between Bolivia and Paraguay was fought in the 1930s over a piece of land between the two countries. Céspedes depicts the conflict as stalemate. His narrative scheme is the diary of a sergeant in charge of a detachment assigned to clear a road in the jungle. Water is scarce and is brought to the men by truck from a considerable distance. As the situation worsens, they begin to think of digging a well, and eventually decide to do so. The diary covers a period of almost eleven months, from January 15 to December 7, 1933. Dates on the several entries help develop a sense of slowly passing time. The narrator's account develops the drudgery of the work, the living death of concentrating on the well in the middle of the jungle. As they dig deeper and deeper without finding water, it becomes apparent that the well is a metaphor of the war. If this aware-ness does not develop gradually, it must come suddenly when the sergeant and his men decide to give up, but are ordered by an officer to keep on digging. They never find water.

The conflict on the level of narration is between success and failure. On a deeper level it is between life and death. Appropriately, the author shifts reference in the narration from water to war. To explain how this shift takes place means revealing the outcome, not a desirable step in the analysis of a story, but necessary in this instance. The Paraguayan enemy believes that the well is functional and decides to take it. The Bolivian detachment defends the hole in the ground as if it were really valuable, and several soldiers of both sides are killed. Then, in an ironic ending the well does prove to have a limited value because it serves as a grave for the men killed in battle. There is a further irony in the fact that the detachment began the well in a depression left from an earlier attempt, and of course left an even deeper depression to be found by those destined to come later on.

Cespedes's narration is consistently from the sergeant's point of view. There is some dialogue, but the narrative situation does not create the problem involving speech peculiarities that exists in many *criollista* stories, especially those with an *indigenista* slant.

This story about the Chaco War inevitably suggests the large body of literature about the Mexican Revolution, which was an entirely different kind of military—and social—action, and which certainly brings to the foreground a complex of questions concerning the value of the human individual and the meaning of violence. Among the many *cuentistas* of the Revolution, Rafael Muñoz (Mexico, 1899–1972) stands out because of his transformation of story material. Most writers on this subject floundered to some degree with regard to how much the referent should be transformed. Their material came from direct experience or from knowing someone who had experienced the Revolution directly. Luis Leal states that, in the case of Muñoz, one cannot tell where history ends and fiction begins.[4] The value of the human individual is absolutely central in Muñoz's "Oro, caballo y hombre" (1933; Gold, Horse and Man), about the death of the leader Rodolfo Fierro, whose concern for the death of others never exceeded zero degree.

Fictional treatment of the Revolution promoted attention to social problems and the value of human life, even when the stories did not deal specifically with the war's military aspects. A famous work by Jorge Ferretis (Mexico, 1902–1962), "Hombres en tempestad" (1941; Men Against the Storm), places a higher value on the life of an ox than on the life of a human being. It deals with the stark economic reality that some people face, and emphasizes the minimal quality of life that is portrayed in many stories of social relevance. Probably the most heartwarming treatment of such impoverishment to be found in Spanish American literature is Arturo Uslar Pietri's (Venezuela, 1905–   ) "La lluvia" (1936; Rain), a story that combines earthy reality with an element of fantasy.

"La lluvia" opens in the house of a rural couple at a moment when the wife thinks she hears rain. The story takes place during a drought; this condition is frequent in Spanish American letters and may be of symbolic as well as literal significance. In Uslar Pietri's story, it is specifically symbolic of the arid marriage of Jesuso and Usebia. She is mistaken about the rain, and the first scene is one of desperate pessimism. When Usebia goes out into the field, she finds a boy who seems to have no background at all and who becomes a member of the household. His presence brings meaning into the lives of Jesuso and Usebia as he gives them a reason to look beyond themselves and into the future.

The boy is a metaphor of rain. His presence is to the marriage as rain is to the earth, but the association is even more complicated because rain itself affects the marriage. The relationship of the boy to the earth is not as apparent; however, there is a suggestion of a relationship when Usebia discovers him among the furrows, playing a game that involves urinating. Seymour Menton considers this association fundamental to the meaning of the story, and relates the association of boy with water to his unexplained appearance and disappearance.[5] It is interesting that the narrator never resolves the mystery of the boy. Since no practical explanation of his role ever appears, one naturally accepts it as belonging to the realm of the marvellous, but the narrator makes very little of it.

Uslar Pietri's story has two main components—the living conditions of the couple, and the state of their marriage. It is natural to accept the former as characteristic of a certain area, but the real emphasis is on the marital problem, giving the story a universal meaning in conjunction with its regionalistic cultural background.

Regionalism and cosmopolitanism in literature often function together, although one or the other may be dominant at any given point. During a substantial part of the 1930s (from about 1933 until the end of the decade) regionalism does seem to dominate, but its coexistence with universal meaning, in "La lluvia," suggests the continuation of cosmopolitanism, and Eduardo Mallea's "Conversación" (1936) strongly confirms cosmopolitanism's continued presence. This is one of several Mallea stories set in metropolitan Buenos Aires. The setting makes the story nonrural by definition, and this fact prohibits its being regionalistic, if we assume that regionalism must be rural or at least provincial. However, it is important to realize that Mallea's story material is very familiar to him, probably more familiar than some rural situations were to the authors who dealt with them. In fact, the functional meaninglessness of the lives portrayed in the story may reflect a kind of alienation which, at that time, was peculiar (regionalistic) to Buenos Aires.

Mallea uses a detailed setting and a limited amount of action. Emphasis is on the conversation. The opening words of the story are "He didn't answer," which is really anticonversation and, through its negativism sets the tone of a story in which nothing really matters. Gradually the protagonists reveal their personalities and we learn that they are a couple who, though not entirely isolated in society, find very little that is important in what goes on around them. Indeed, on this level of understanding, the conflict may be most accurately expressed as significance versus triviality, or abstractly, meaning versus meaninglessness. Translated into its deepest metaphor, the conflict is simply life versus death.

Their conversation reveals, in three stages, the lack of concern that characterizes their attitudes. The three stages, interestingly enough, would represent for most people three areas of ascending importance, but for Mallea's protagonists, all are equally meaningless. The first is centered on the two protagonists' selves. He gallantly informs her that she looks better in a different dress. The reader who expects a violent reaction on her part is in for a surprise. She simply agrees with him, and the ensuing bits of conversation indicate that she really doesn't care what he thinks. They are not fighting; it simply is not important. The second stage involves the couple's relationship with friends; what they say is partly nagging, partly lack of concern. Then a paperboy appears. The man buys a paper and meaninglessness moves to the third stage, that of world affairs. They find that the news is the same as always, and soon shift attention back to themselves. After dining in a restaurant, they decide to go home because there really is no place to go or anything to do.

Recapitulating the experience of "Conversación" and "La lluvia," it is astonishing how similar the conflict developed by Mallea is to that in Uslar Pietri's story. The settings make the stories appear different superficially, and of course there is a real difference in "La lluvia" because the boy functions as an agent of resolution, whereas there is neither agent nor resolution in "Conversación." The short story in the last half of the

1930s has become less dependent on the tricky plot, the dramatic climax, and the ironic twist. This tendency is apparent not only in the two stories compared here, but also in "Una cáscara en la banqueta," "La plaza de las carretas," and "Warma Kukay."

Return to Innovation and Cosmopolitanism: The Early 1940s

In 1939 María Luisa Bombal (Chile, 1910–1980) published "El árbol" ("The Tree"), a key work in Spanish American literature. This story confirms and strengthens the kind of narrative represented earlier by "Conversación" and earlier still by "Tachas." From the publication of "El árbol," the regionalism—cosmopolitanism pendulum swings again toward the latter.

Bombal tells the story of a rare personality—a woman who is outwardly unsure of herself, but who, deep within, knows exactly who she is and what she wants. The story is framed by a piano recital attended by Brígida, the protagonist; the music by Mozart, Beethoven, and Chopin, in that order, corresponds to different stages in her life, evoking memories that are intensely confessional, narrated in third person. The story is what Brígida experiences; the reality develops as she sees it. Bombal very unobtrusively furnishes the reader some important information near the beginning of the story: that Brígida is not an intellectual but she is a very sensitive person, that she is separated from her husband, and that he is older than she. This information evokes the questions, are these facts related to each other and, if so, how?

The exposition in "El árbol" includes information about Brígida's childhood, so the story covers a considerable number of years. As the narrator concentrates on answering those questions, there is no feeling that excess information is being offered. As a small child, the protagonist lived in a situation that laid the foundation of her personality, and the narrative conflict is between her deep emotion and her inability to express what she feels.

This unusual little girl eventually marries one of her father's friends. Thus the conflict, while remaining basically the same, now metamorphoses into her passion versus her husband's reserve. Brígida's disappointment turns into resignation and the conflict then is best described as her desire for excitement instead of the calm that she decides is her fate. This condition does not last, however, and she develops a private life, a world of her own that functions with reference to what she sees from the window of her dressing room and focuses on a tree that becomes symbolic of the joys that are absent from her real life but present in her dreams. The alterations of narrative conflict that reflect Brígida's feelings have taken place as follows: deep emotion to passion to desire for excitement to life in her imaginary world. On the side involving her husband, the stages are inability to express herself to husband's reserve to calm resignation to unsatisfactory love life.

With the destruction of her imaginary world Brígida is finally able to say, at least in her own way, what she has been unable to express; at which point the two lines of conflict coincide. As Bombal brings the story to an end, it no longer matters whether Brígida's ultimate expressive self-realization happens before the recital or as a result of the memories stimulated by the music. "El árbol" makes an interesting comparison with "La lluvia" and "Conversación." In still a third social context, it is the story of a couple in a troubled relationship, of conflict between meaning and meaninglessness. As the boy in "La lluvia" acts as an agent of resolution, in "El árbol," the imaginary life of the protagonist functions in a similar way.

It is quite accurate—and probably useful—to refer to "El árbol" as a pyschological story, but that is not a satisfactory generic term. Hernández Catá's "Noventa días" may also be called psychological, but it is an entirely different kind of story, more like Madame Bovary, with the narrative clearly developed. "El árbol" takes the reader inside the making of the narrative. This difference is characteristic of many stories of this period and it is created by changes in narrative strategy, even in the attitude of the author toward fiction, rather than by innovations in subject matter or theme. Speaking of Efrén Hernández, Luis Leal says the author is more interested in the simple pleasure of narrating than in telling what happens.[6] This quality is apparent in "Tachas" and is even more important in a later story, "Cerrazón sobre Nicomaco" (1946; Nicomaco Closed In), in which the narrator directs himself specifically to his readers (or listeners) while in the act of narrating, refers to himself as "I" and also as "Nicomaco," and comments frequently on the act of narrating the story. For example: "Let us blow, as time blows upon our lives, let us blow upon the edge of the notebook made of these pages. Let unread pages turn; unread and unwritten, let the pages turn." Or an entirely different kind of reference: "Between the preceding line and this one, a real eternity intervenes."

Hernández has the ability to be funny and absolutely serious at the same time. There are moments when his stories seem surrealistic. His narrator-protagonists are amusingly self-deprecatory. Nicomaco, in one part of the story, satirizes the inconsequential bureaucrat in his own person. But the story also has its tragic side, and although one may not always be quite certain what is going on in "Cerrazón sobre Nicomaco," it seems fairly safe to assume a case of paranoia, or possible masochism. It ends with the protagonist's account of a repeated dream of being closed in, but by his own effort. Clearly, this is a psychological story of still a different kind.

It is well to mention Juan Bosch (Dominican Republic, 1909–   ) at this point because his work is decidedly *criollista,* and his presence is a reminder that the literary pendulum has not swung all the way to one end of its arc. Bosch's best known story is "La mujer" (1933; The Woman) which excels in narrative structure of two carefully balanced criss-crossing themes and concludes with an ironic twist that seemed stranger three decades ago than it does now.[7] The irony is that a woman kills the man who defends her against an abusive husband. The theme was not new in literature, but was generally taken to be characteristic of an identifiable socioeconomic circumstance.

Bosch is a realist *cuentista,* a good one, but different from the majority of more innovative writers of the 1940s. "La mujer" was published in the mid 1930s and is quite appropriate to that time; however, Bosch continued to write in a similar manner while the short story, as a genre, was developing in other directions. "Dos pesos de agua" ("Two Dollars' Worth of Water") was published in 1941. The material is folkloric and the setting is another drought. It also contains an element of fantasy and an ironic twist. The principal character is a woman who refuses to leave her farm in spite of the drought. An outside narrator tells her story and inserts the fantastic element that she could not know.

As her neighbors leave one by one, she gives each two pesos for the souls in purgatory, in exchange for rain. The fantastic elements enter in the form of a scene in purgatory in which the council regrets having overlooked all this prepayment and decides to make just retribution. Since even one gift of two pesos is much larger than any other single gift, the accumulated funds pay for an excessive amount of rain. The theme of the story gives it a tone of legend, and this effect is enhanced by the scene in purgatory. The end is tragic, not simply because of the rain itself, but because the woman's immeasurable faith causes her to lose everything.

Lino Novás Calvo (Cuba, 1905–   ) deals with humble people in an entirely different way. While maintaining a keen awareness of the unfortunate circumstances and attitudes that may affect their lives, his own attitude as a *cuentista* allows him to see them as a part of society rather than as alienated from it. For the most part, he accomplishes this difference by manipulating the point of view, that is, who is seeing what we are told, rather than whose voice is telling it.

His "No le sé decil" (1946; I Don't Know What to Say) presents a peasant's dilemma through the eyes of a compassionate physician. Novás Calvo's narration seems straightforward; it opens with some necessary background, then suggests the character of the physician before beginning the action. Much of the interest in the story is created by withholding information while he develops the characters of the peasants whose standard response is, "No le sé decil." The physician suffers the frustration caused by this inability or disinclination to communicate. In turn, his attempts to help are limited when his old Ford ambulance gets stuck on a country road. Two women whose husbands are engaged in a knife fight have come to him for help, but give him little information. Their hermetic character is emphasized when they remain stolidly seated in the ambulance while the doctor tries to extricate the mired wheel.

The conflict in "No le sé decil" is especially interesting because on the first level of awareness it is life versus death, and it is the same on the deepest level. Between these two levels, there are several contrasts, created by different incidents, that are interesting variations on the basic conflict. The life-versus-death contrast is mirrored in the difference between actvity and resignation. When the two women come to the doctor for help, even that small act is something of a victory for him. Other metaphors of the contrast are communication versus "no le sé decil," the ambulance in motion versus the ambulance mired, and the active physician versus the stoic women.

Novás Calvo's story material may be either rural or urban; whatever the setting, the central incident is supported by interesting characterization. "No le sé decil" portrays the uncommunicative aspect of the peasant personality, but it suggests a full characterization of the doctor even though only a few details are made explicit. In "'Aliados' y 'Alemanes'" (1946; 'Allies' and 'Germans') the central event is an act of vandalism provoked by the rivalry between drivers of the old carriages in Havana and drivers of new Ford taxis. The enormous appeal of this story, however, is created by the narrator who remembers the rivalry when he was a boy and was involved with both sides of the fight. We know what the narrator knows and the author scrupulously avoids revealing more. Another story, "La noche de Ramón Yendía" (1942; "The Dark Night of Ramón Yendía"), is a terrifying chase, both psychological and real. Novás Calvo creates an intimate mood of terror by combining exterior narration with passages in stream of consciousness.

Cuentistas in the 1940s used both rural and urban story material without making one seem more regionalistic than the other. Novás Calvo's urban stories are as typical of a time and place as "No le sé decil." Familiarity with the story material and narrative strategies that cultivate the reader's sensitivity to detailed characterization are primary qualities in his work, just as they are in Bombal's "El árbol." Similar qualities are apparent in José Revueltas's (Mexico, 1914–1976) "La soledad" (1944; Solitude). It is important to note that, while "El árbol" and "La soledad" are less related to a specific place than any of the three stories by Novás Calvo, they are clearly related to a time when anguish or alienation was the most frequently discussed characteristic of modern individuals.

"La soledad" opens in the middle of a sentence: ". . . with the desk sergeant," from a fragment of dialogue. Immediately the narrator's voice makes us aware of the sergeant himself, and tells us how he perceived the spoken words. Once this point of view is established—almost immediately—Revueltas maintains it throughout the story. The officer is referred to by his title rather than by a personal name, yet a large part of the story concerns his difficulty associating self-awareness with his identity as desk sergeant. A man who claims to be a murderer makes contact with the officer, who, throughout the story, is continually aware of the problem of identity, of the commitment of individuals to each other, and of the relationship of doing to being. The conflict between individual identity and alienation persists until the end of the story, at which point the officer signs a report with his name, not merely his title.

Revueltas is one of the most versatile cuentistas in Latin America. His settings and narrative procedures vary so greatly that he is not easily classifiable. "El encuentro" (1940; Encounter, or perhaps, Discovery) is an especially poignant story in which one unfortunate person establishes a relationship with another outcast. The setting is a small town, although it does not matter what town it may be, or even whether it is a neighborhood in a large city. In this very short work, unusual behavior or unusual ugliness places a character in the role of outcast. Revueltas depicts one of the principals from the point of view of other people in the town; he shows the other principal from the narrator's point of view, but describes how the people reacted to her. This difference serves as an identifying device in the brief characterizations.

A third Revueltas story, "Dios en la tierra" (1944; God On This Earth), is very different, but no less typical of the author's work. It is more easily understood if one knows something of Mexican history. In the 1920s the anticlerical policies of the Mexican government were militantly confronted by religious traditionalists, with the consequent atrocities that religious wars often inspire. Religious traditionalism was a popular sentiment, so the federal soldiers were not always enthusiastic about enforcing the law. Public school teachers were often in the position of being enemies of the people because they represented the progressive attitude of the government. "Dios en la tierra" tells the story of a detachment of federal soldiers who are in enemy territory where they are denied water. They face the people's hate or, as Revueltas puts it, "The town was closed with hate and stones." The story focuses on this hate and the evil it creates, the suffering of the soldiers and the brutal murder of the teacher who tried to help them. Revueltas uses metaphors of dryness or hardness, and constantly repeats the word God. Although no one could avoid feeling sympathy for those who are mistreated, this story depends not on characterization but on an idea—the notion of religious fanaticism; while it is not essay, it does convey a message. Characters are used to bring the notion to life, rather than to reflect a human condition.

Jorge Luis Borges (1899–   ) does something similar in "El Sur" (1944; "The South"). This story has nothing to do with a religious war, but is based on a notion that, again, is better understood if one knows something about Argentina. Although it is an uneasy comparison, one may reasonably say that the South in Argentina has many of the connotations that the West has in the United States—adventure, manliness, escape from urban dreariness, and freedom. Borges tells the story of a very unadventurous man in Buenos Aires who goes South, either in reality or in illusion, and is trapped into an immediate demonstration of his prowess as a fighter. The characterization deals with two aspects of the man, his quiet self and the frontiersman. He is the personification of the idea of going South.

Much of the charm of "El Sur" comes from the skill with which the story is constructed. One cannot be certain what is reality and what is illusion. It is important to recognize Borges's insistence on making a good fiction, especially since many modern cuentistas have tended to deemphasize the clever fiction in favor of perceptive characterization. It might seem, therefore, that Borges is no more than a literary reactionary looking back toward past masters of the short story, but that is the case only to a limited extent. He is indeed well informed in the tradition of the genre, and he readily admits his special interest in several writers. Borges does more than cultivate the carefully made story, however; he persistently bases his works on notions or concepts that turn out to be of more enduring interest than the characters as individual people.

"Las ruinas circulares" (1944; "The Circular Ruins"), unlike "El Sur," is not only based on a concept, it is based on one that is not related to the reality in which Borges lives. The author might have known a person like the protagonist of "El Sur," and he certainly knows the concepts behind both stories, but he does not know a philosopher who decided to dream another man into existence only to discover that he is himself the product of another's dream. "Las ruinas circulares" is a wonderful story that can be read and enjoyed on different levels or within different frames of reference. There is a basic reading that begins with a sense of mysterious origin, flirts with reality, and finally discovers the trick in the story. A "mythic" reading may begin with a sense of primordial reality, progress through an ordering of chaos, and end with the knowledge that the source and the product are of the same order. A metafictional reading may find this to be the story of the creative act. In the final analysis, all the readings are one—the experience of the story itself, and this experience is the narration of a concept.

"Las ruinas circulares" is a long way from Quiroga's "La gallina degollada," and there may be echoes of "Juan Darién" as far as narration of a concept is concerned; Borges is as pleased to surprise us in "Las ruinas circulares" as Quiroga is at the end of "La gallina degollada." From Quiroga to Borges, the Spanish American short story exploits many themes and variations, and is characterized by fascinating experiments in the strategies of narrating. Perhaps Borges himself is the one to write the history of this genre that is always changing, but is always the same.

John S. Brushwood

University of Kansas, Lawrence

THE SPANISH AMERICAN SHORT STORY FROM BORGES TO THE PRESENT

George R. McMurray

1940–1949: New Directions

Since 1940 the Spanish American short story has displayed a growing diversity in its development. In general, the genre has become increasingly sophisticated, its universal themes and experimental techniques having served to reflect the complex realities of today's rapidly changing world. The tendencies toward universality and experimentation can be traced in part to sociohistorical factors such as the arrival in Spanish America of many highly educated European immigrants during World War II, the unprecedented growth of urban centers, and progress in public education, which has created a larger and more intellectually oriented reading public. At the same time it should be pointed out that most contemporary Spanish American writers remain committed to the betterment of their underdeveloped, strife-ridden societies, although their ideology is often embedded in the texture of their creations.

A logical starting point for a discussion of contemporary Spanish American short fiction is the work of the Argentine Jorge Luis Borges whose metaphysical tales of the 1940s gave birth to a new literary era. Written in a highly compressed, classical style with an occasional baroque twist, these tales present a series of hallucinatory, although hauntingly real, visions of the absurd human experience. Perhaps Borges's most significant metaphysical *ficción* is "Tlön, Uqbar, Orbis Tertius" (1941; "Tlön, Uqbar, Orbis Tertius"), a combination story and essay about a planet named Tlön, which although described at length in an encyclopedia, turns out to be the invention of a group of scholars. Tlön is presented as a complete cosmos governed by strict, carefully formulated, but provisional laws based on philosophical idealism, that is, the belief that material objects are ideas in our minds, with no independent existence. Since the inhabitants of Tlön conceive of the universe as a series of mental processes, it is not surprising that their language has no nouns for material objects, nor that psychology has become their principal scientific discipline. The appearance of philosophical materialism and pantheism in their midst scandalizes them, but as the years pass they gradually accept certain tenets of these heretical philosophies, thus demonstrating the provisional nature of laws formulated by man. The story ends on an ironic note when two material objects (a compass from Tlön and a heavy, cone-shaped statue representing a Tlönian deity) make their appearance in the real world, and the inhabitants of Earth become fascinated with an encyclopedia describing the well-ordered, though fictitious, planet. Meanwhile, the story's skeptical narrator, whom we are tempted to identify with Borges, remains indifferent to the new philosophy, realizing that it is just another chapter in the ever-evolving history of ideas.

The reflection of an encyclopedia in a mirror at the beginning of the story provides an opening into its labyrinthine structure as well as a clue to its meaning. Borges suggests that just as mirrors reproduce illusions of reality, encyclopedic knowledge is nothing more than an illusory mirror of the human mind, a vast, but well-ordered labyrinth that stands in sharp contrast to the undecipherable labyrinth of the real world. Thus the encyclopedia of Tlön emerges as a reflection of a reflection, all of which suggests that for human beings reality is not what things are but how they see them artificially categorized and distorted by logic. Like all of Borges's metaphysical tales, "Tlön, Uqbar, Orbus Tertius" negates reason by subverting objective reality and replacing it with a poetically conceived, hallucinatory creation of language. As we shall see in "La muerte y la brújula" and "El Aleph," irony and the magic of art constitute Borges's principal weapons against a world he can neither organize nor understand.

"La muerte y la brújula" (1944; "Death and the Compass") is another of Borges's seminal works, primarily because of its presentation of life as an absurd labyrinth created by human reason. A compelling detective story with profound philosophical implications and ironic overtones, this tale tells of a duel of wits between a clever sleuth named Erik

Lönnrot and an equally clever gangster, Red Scharlach. The plot describes a series of murders, the first of which induces the "pure reasoner," Lönnrot, to immerse himself in the study of the cabala to discover the culprit. This arcane subject, which fascinates Lönnrot but actually has nothing to do with the crime, brings him face to face with Scharlach who, it turns out, has set a trap for him all along.

"La muerte y la brújula" dramatizes not only the limits of reason, but its pitfalls. Lönnrot is doomed from the beginning because, as Treviranus (the simple-minded police commissioner) surmises, the first murder is the result of chance, an element Lönnrot rejects out of hand. Thus his efforts to solve the crime as he would a mind-boggling puzzle lead him into a diamond-shaped labyrinth that parodies the reasoning mind's fragmented view of random reality and, at the same time, suggests the absurdity of the confrontation between man and the irreducible world. As in several of Borges's tales, the climax occurs when the rationalistic protagonist meets his double, or alter ego, and falls victim to annihilation. Indeed, Lönnrot and Scharlach are more than likely meant to be doubles. Not only are their names similar (*rot* and *scharlach* mean red in German), but their minds function with the same rigid logic. Moreover, their antithetical natures, or inverted mirror images, are demonstrated by their roles as detective/criminal and pursuer/pursued, roles that ultimately become ironically reversed.

Metaphysical irony, or a striving man's defeat by a supreme being plotting against him, is another major ingredient. As D. P. Gallagher has stated[1], the story could be read as a fable about a man (Lönnrot) who attempts to explain God's (Scharlach's) deeds without suspecting that he is doomed from the start because God has placed him in a labyrinth, granting him limited success and then invalidating it by killing him. Lönnrot remains a prisoner of reason even in the face of death, plotting his afterlife duel of wits with Scharlach along a straight line, a reference to the maze described by Zeno of Elea[2] and here a metaphor of eternity. The title also anticipates the ironic ending because it is the compass, an instrument designed to guide its user to safety, that leads Lönnrot to Triste-le-Roy where he meets Red Scharlach and his tragic fate.

"La muerte y la brújula" parodies the modern detective story, Lönnrot bringing to mind the brilliant Sherlock Holmes and Treviranus the plodding Dr. Watson. It is a masterpiece of short fiction because it deftly fuses form and content; that is, its convoluted structure conveys the theme that for reasoning man, life is an absurd labyrinth designed more by chance than by logic. This theme of the absurd, which receives more detailed attention in connection with "El guardagujas" (1952), by Juan José Arreola, becomes a major element in subsequent Spanish American fiction.

"El Aleph" (1949; "The Aleph") is perhaps Borges's finest example of self-conscious metafiction, a work in which the creative process itself, or the technique of writing a story, becomes the subject matter. In addition to describing Borges's esthetic concerns, this well-known tale presents some of his basic philosophical preoccupations and his ironic view of the Argentine literary scene. The first-person-narrator, who refers to himself as Borges and who will be referred to as the fictional Borges, is still grieving over the death of his beloved Beatriz Viterbo. Each year to commemorate her birthday he pays a visit to the home of her cousin, Carlos Argentino Danieri, a pompous, mediocre poet who is writing a long descriptive poem entitled "The Earth." His inspiration for this poem is the Aleph, a magical disk-shaped object he has discovered in his cellar and which contains a simultaneous vision of the entire world. (We are told in the story's epilogue that the Aleph is the first letter of the Hebrew alphabet and that for the cabalists it signifies limitless, pure divinity.) When Argentino shows the Aleph to the fictional Borges, the latter is thoroughly dazzled by it, but refuses to discuss the marvelous object because in it he discovers some obscene letters written to Argentino by Beatriz.

When the fictional Borges attempts to describe the Aleph, he experiences a sense of inadequacy because the all-encompassing vision he saw was simultaneous, and language is a lineal medium. Or, as the real Borges has stated on several occasions, reality is not verbal. Thus unlike the pompous Argentino, the fictional Borges forgets the Aleph, realizing that his linguistic description of it is inferior to its visible reality. Time soon erodes his memory of it just as it has eroded his memory of Beatriz's face. The real Borges, however, succeeds ingeniously in creating a symbolic Aleph, which as we shall see, not only surpasses the original in subtlety, but outlasts it.

Even the most casual reader will perceive certain parallels between the Aleph and Beatriz, both having been described at some length, and with the passage of time, both having faded from the fictional Borges's memory. (Beatriz is first presented in Argentino's home when the narrator gazes fondly at pictures taken of her during various stages of her life. Subsequently she is described by the fictional Borges, and finally the total vision of her is rounded out in his mind when he sees her obscene letters and her corpse in the Aleph.)

Although this vision of Beatriz is lost by the fictional Borges (the narrator), for both the real Borges and the reader it not only retains its totality but acquires a special significance. The real Borges, understanding that he can never capture the simultaneous vision of the Aleph in sequential language, creates the total picture of Beatriz within the story as a symbolic version of the Aleph. It is a version that the reader must grasp intuitively by combining all the story's parts into a simultaneous view of the whole. Thus the total fictional impression corresponds to the impression of totality conveyed to the fictional Borges by the Aleph. In fact, the symbolic Aleph (the story of Beatriz) is superior to Argentino's Aleph (which is destroyed when his house is torn down) because as a work of art it overcomes the limitations of language and conveys a permanent, intuited reality that transcends the barriers of logic and negates the erosion of chronologic time.

"El Aleph" can also be read as an example of the metafictional story that feeds on another literary work to create its own essence, the other work in this case being Dante's *The Divine Comedy*. One of Carlos Argentino Daneri's surnames combines the names of the medieval Italian poet; because Carlos Argentino leads Borges to the Aleph in his cellar, he can also be identified with Virgil, Dante's guide in the "Inferno;" and Beatriz Viterbo recalls Dante's beloved, not only because of her name, but also because during her lifetime she treated Borges with disdain, just as Beatrice treated Dante disdainfully in Paradise. These parallels serve to enrich the literary texture of Borges's story which, when read in this light, becomes a vast work of art in miniature, just as the Aleph represents the entire world in miniature. "El Aleph" is a story about a story; its themes are the elusiveness of reality and the efforts of an author (the real Borges) to capture this reality symbolically. The fact that this tale exists in the web of *The Divine Comedy* lends it an aura of myth and suggests that, given the inability of language to represent reality, the only stories that can be written are stories about fiction.

"Tlön, Uqbar, Orbus Tertius," "La muerte y la brújula," and "El Aleph" all dramatize the negation of reason; the first parodies encyclopedic knowledge and philosophical systems; the second underscores the role of chance in determining human destiny; and the third demonstrates the superiority of intuitive art over mimetic realism as a means of capturing a reality eroded by time. Together these tales synthesize the principal elements of Borges's Weltanschauung and esthetics.

About the same time that Borges was creating his metaphysical fantasies, the Uruguayan Juan Carlos Onetti (1909–   ) began writing short fiction that in some respects resembles that of the Argentine master. Onetti's "Un sueño realizado" (written in 1941, published in a collection in 1951; "A Dream Come True") is narrated by a retired theater director, Langman, who recalls that many years previously, at the request of a strange, middle-aged woman, he organized a single performance of a play based on a dream she described to him. The story and the play end simultaneously when the woman, having portrayed a youthful version of herself in her "sueño realizado," died on the stage. Like Borges, Onetti reveals a marked preoccupation with time; both depict psychological doubles; and just as the imaginary planet of Tlön becomes fused with the narrator's world, the woman's play and Langman's tale ultimately become one and the same.

"Un sueño realizado" also illustrates the surrealists' search for a certain point in the mind where life and death, past and future, and reality and imagination cease to be perceived as contradictions. Onetti's fusion of opposites creates an aura of ambiguity, often tinged with irony, that dominates the content as well as the structural patterning of his tale. For example, the mocking allusions to *Hamlet* expressed by Blanes (one of Langman's actors) becomes a leitmotiv suggesting the artistic perfection Langman will never achieve as well as the work-within-a-work technique that in both Shakespeare's tragedy and Onetti's story reveals a climatic moment of truth. (Hamlet discovers his uncle's guilt in the same way that Onetti reveals the tragic reality of life.) The woman is portrayed through a series of striking contradictions, first being described as middle-aged, threatened by physical decay, and mad, and subsequently as youthful, childlike, and strange but not demented. Blanes informs Langman that the woman wants to relive her dream because it gave her a moment of happiness, although, he adds, the word "happiness" may not accurately describe her feelings. In the final lines, after the woman's unexpected demise, Langman enigmatically states that he understood what she was searching for, that "it was all clear, like one of those things you know as a child but later on find words are useless to explain." By reenacting her dream, the woman probably hoped to escape from the drab reality she, like Blanes and Langman, found increasingly intolerable. Onetti's response to her dilemma is the dramatization of a past moment of happiness (her dream) followed immediately by her death, a juxtaposition of dream and reality that constitutes a surrealistic moment of insight into the absurd human experience.

Alejo Carpentier (1904–1980) of Cuba is another innovator who uses time as a major ingredient in his work. In "Semejante a la noche" (written in 1947, published in a collection in 1958; "Like the Night"), a first-person narrator of shifting identities relates analogous episodes from six moments of history: the Trojan War, the sixteenth-century Spanish conquest of America, the seventeenth-century French expeditions to America, the Crusades, World War I, and World War II. The narrators are all young, inexperienced warriors whose archetypal behavior prior to embarking on their dangerous missions suggests a striking circularity in time and, consequently, a negation of linear history and its implications of progress. Thus both theme and structure are conveyed by a series of motifs, which include the loading of ships, the soldier's exalted pride in his profession, the desire for wealth and glory, the belief in patriotic ideals and religious doctrine, the yearning for last-minute sexual adventures, and the gnawing fear of death.

Given the repetitions of the plot, it may surprise the reader that Carpentier has meticulously documented the historical events he describes. This strengthens his possible intent to prove unequivocally that time is circular and history repetitious. The author's preoccupation with time is further demonstrated by the story's twenty-four-hour framework, the first and final episodes occurring at dawn on consecutive days, and the remaining episodes occurring successively in the morning, at noon, in the afternoon, and at nightfall.

This circular sructure also implies condemnation of war and negation of the invincible hero myth, for through the technique of repetition with variation, noble ideals and patriotic fervor gradually give way to skepticism and cynicism. For example, the initial segment presents an idealized picture of Helen, who must be set free at all cost from her cruel captors; whereas on the final page we are told that the accounts of her mistreatment were propaganda and that the real cause of the war was the desire for economic gain. The last narrator, moreover, is reduced to the role of anti-hero when he finds himself incapable of satisfying the sexual demands of his sweetheart.

Capentier's tale encompasses much of Western civilization: the abrupt temporal dislocations, shifting point of view, and exotic, baroque vocabulary lend a magical, mirror-like quality to the chain of events. The message conveyed by this ingenious montage of historical moments is that although human circumstances may vary from century to century, the human condition remains essentially unchanged.

The Argentine Adolfo Bioy Casares (1914–   ) takes quite a different view of time, using it as a tool to dissolve objective reality and create
his psychological fantasies. Typical of this author's short fiction is "En
memoria de Paulina" (1948; "In Memory of Pauline"), the story of a
young writer (the narrator) who loses his lifelong friend and fiancée
(Paulina) to an aggressive colleague named Julius Montero. On his
return to Argentina after two years of study in London, the narrator has a
fond, if brief and somewhat strange, reunion with Paulina, but the
following day he learns that she had been murdered by Montero on the
eve of his (the narrator's) departure for London. The narrator concludes
that the image of Paulina that appeared to him was not her ghost, but the
monstrous projection of his jealous rival's imagination.

Although Tzvetan Todorov would consider this story an example of
the marvelous, other critics, including Ana María Barrenechea, place it
in the category of the fantastic.[3] Bioy Casares carefully anticipates the
denouement through a series of mysterious, and seemingly insignificant, details that ultimately explain the intriguing temporal discrepan-
cies as well as Paulina's behavior during her last encounter with the
narrator. This hallucinatory vision of Paulina assumes greater plausibil-
ity, however, if Montero is seen as the narrator's inverted mirror image or
antithetical self. The two characters are indeed opposites, the narrator
emerging as shy and highly cultured and Montero (the name means
hunter in Spanish) as vulgar, vigorous, and, in his own words, "a
savage." Although both are writers, the narrator is unsure of his creative
powers and even fears Paulina might discover that he is an "imposter."
By contrast, Montero's self-confidence becomes evident when he bran-
dishes his voluminous manuscript with the air of a tyrant just before
reading it in its entirety to the docile narrator. The term imposter refers to
the narrator's dubious ability as a writer as well as to his inability to
overcome his narcissism—he sees Paulina as a mere reflection of
himself—and prove himself as a lover. Thus he solves his dilemma by
imagining her cruel rejection of him in favor of Montero and, consequently, her tragic fate. Montero's consuming jealousy not only bol-
sters the narrator's deflated ego, but serves as a tool for achieving his
revenge.

The story's underlying irony derives from the narrator's unawareness
of his irrational psychic impulses, a situation that leads him to his
fantastic, but almost logical, explanation of the strange sequence of
events he has envisioned. Like Borges and Onetti, Bioy Casares
dramatizes the instability and disunity of the human personality,

another theme that assumes greater importance in subsequent Spanish American fiction.

1950–1959: Protest and Universality

The most noteworthy writers of short fiction during the 1940s reveal a marked tendency toward universality, emphasizing metaphysical, literary, and psychological themes. By contrast, the works of the 1950s convey a stronger awareness of the political and social problems plaguing much of Spanish America. A case in point is "Espuma y nada más" (1950; "Just Lather, that's All"), by the Colombian Hernando Téllez (1908–1966), a story based on the civil war (*la violencia*) that wracked his native land from 1948 until well into the 1960s. A barber (the first-person narrator) acting as a secret informer for the rebel cause describes his distraught state of mind on finding himself obliged to shave an army officer, Captain Torres, who has resorted to torture and mass executions to quell the guerrilla forces in the region. The story ends with an ironic twist that alters its esthetic form as well as its overall meaning.

"Espuma y nada más" is a masterfully structured tale that owes its tautness and climactic denouement to its subtly conceived characters and its various levels of conflict. The most obvious of these is the psychological duel between the two antithetical antagonists. Because the story is told almost entirely in the words of the barber, the reader witnesses his inner tension as he attempts to mask cowardice with professional pride, reminding himself that his duty to shave Torres to perfection precludes cutting his throat as the rebels would expect of him. An entire community in conflict is evoked when the narrator imagines that were he to kill Torres, he would be proclaimed a hero by some and by others a murderer.

Irony, the story's major structural element, is a balancing device that modifies opposites and shapes the reader's response. Thus throughout much of the narrator's monologue the reader tends to sympathize with him and loathe the brutal Torres, assuming, like the narrator, that Torres is unaware of the narrator's activities with the underground. As he leaves the barbershop, however, Torres reveals that he came there to find out whether the narrator would kill him. At this moment both the narrator and the reader become victims of irony, realizing that Torres has deliberately courted danger and, like the typical Latin macho, remained stoically calm in its presence. In this light, Torres elicits a measure of respect, while, by comparison, the weak, razor-wielding narrator is seen as an anti-hero. The lather referred to in the title probably symbolizes the narrator's empty talk of blood revenge and his incapacity for decisive action.

As indicated, the philosophy of the Absurd began to manifest itself in the Spanish American short story during and immediately following World War II. According to Albert Camus, this concept stems from the clash between reasoning man and the unreasonable world, which ignores his quest for the meaning of life. An awakening to the Absurd occurs when the individual, suddenly aware of the lack of purpose in his daily routine, asks himself the crucial question, "Why?" An excellent fictional representation of Camus's philosophy is "El guardagujas" (1952; "The Switchman") by Juan José Arreola (1918–   ), who is occasionally referred to as Mexico's Borges. In this often-anthologized tale a stranger burdened with a heavy suitcase arrives at a deserted station at the exact hour his train is supposed to leave for his destination, "T." As he gazes impatiently at the tracks that seem to melt away in the distance, an old man (the switchman) carrying a tiny red lantern appears from out of nowhere and proceeds to relate to the horrified stranger a series of preposterous anecdotes illustrating the unreliability of the train service in that country and suggesting to him that boarding the train is more important than worrying about a precise destination. In the final lines of the story the far-off whistle of a train is heard, but on inquiring again where the stranger wants to go, the switchman receives the answer "X" instead of "T." At this moment the old man vanishes, leaving only the tiny light of his lantern bobbing up and down before the noisily approaching locomotive.

"El guardagujas" is rife with symbols that convey its philosophical meaning and determine its esthetic form. The railroad journey can be construed as a metaphor of life and the act of boarding the train as an acceptance of its challenges and uncertainties. The stranger is a non-Absurd man at the beginning of the story; his heavy suitcase represents the burden of reason he carries around with him. The railroad tracks melting away in the distance, however, symbolize the uncertain destiny he will eventually accept, and the fact that deceased travelers are taken, without fail, to the station directed by their tickets denotes death as man's only definite, predetermined destination, a fundamental Absurdist idea.

In an amusing anecdote, the old man describes what happened when a train arrived at an abyss over which no bridge had been constructed. Instead of turning back, the passengers took the train apart and carried it piece by piece to the other side where they reassembled it and continued their journey. In Camus's terms these passengers represent Absurd heroes whose revolt against the Absurd must take the form of action. The stranger's change of destination from "T" to "X" at the end of the story, moreover, indicates his acceptance of the Absurd unknown. The fact that here he is referred to for the first time as the traveler instead of the stranger underscores his newly acquired role as a man (committed to the struggle against chaotic reality) with the potential of becoming a hero like the passengers who carried the train across the abyss.

The stranger's transformation, the mysterious disappearance of the switchman, and the train's arrival, set the stage for the ensuing Absurd journey. It would seem that the tiny lantern confronting the oncoming train symbolizes the clash between limited human reason and the world's dark forces of destruction. It would seem also that the title of the story refers not only to a railroad switchman, but to a kind of catalyst whose role is to awaken the protagonist to his condition and switch him onto another track. Finally, it is likely that the switchman represents the stranger's alter ego, and the entire story a metaphor of existential man's awakening to Camus's question, "Why?"

On an esthetic level, the symbol imagery and structural balance of Arreola's tale demonstrate his attempt to give artistic coherence to the elusive reality that he, as an Absurd creator, finds unacceptable. Thus when the tension between the stranger and his alter ego is finally dissolved, it is replaced immediately by the confrontation between the traveler and his destiny, a destiny rendered absurd by the tiny lantern of reason that appropriately frames the story.

The two leading Mexican writers of the 1950s, Arreola and Juan Rulfo (1918–   ), are exponents of very different literary trends. As we have seen, the former is the creator of highly amusing imaginary works based on ideas taken from a broad cultural spectrum; the latter is a pessimistic, hermetic portrayer of rural life in his native state of Jalisco. Despite their regional settings and sordid, naturalistic themes, however, Rulfo's stories, somewhat in the manner of Faulkner's, attain universal status by exposing the inner lives of their protagonists and thus the core of all humanity.

Rulfo makes effective use of the interior monologue in several of his works, one of these being "Es que somos muy pobres" (1953; "We're Very Poor"). The unnamed child narrator describes a series of disasters that has befallen his peasant family: the recent death of an aunt, a flood that carries away a cow given to his sister Tacha by her father for her dowry, and the ruin of two older sisters who have become prostitutes. In view of these events, the story's initial sentence, "Everything is going from bad to worse here," would seem to imply that for the narrator and his family, life is fraught with misfortunes greater than death. This tragic vision of the world is underscored by their fatalistic acceptance of adversity, perhaps a result of their symbiotic relationship with hostile nature. A series of parallels serves not only to convey this intricate relationship, but to give esthetic coherence to a narrative that might otherwise lack structural unity. Just as the river carries off the highly prized cow, her legs in the air, the two older sisters are led astray by sexual passion, "rolling around on the ground, all naked, and each one with a man on top of her"; on separate occasions the narrator and his mother utter the same phrase ("May God watch over them"), the narrator referring to his sister's cow and her missing calf, and his mother to her two wayward daughters. In the last scene the sobbing Tacha is linked to both her cow and her sisters, her face covered with streams of dirty water, "as if the river had gotten inside her," and her maturing breasts bouncing up and down, starting her "on the road to ruin."

The point of view serves to re-create rather than merely to recount the feelings of the narrator, thus drawing the reader to the center of the action and involving him more directly. Rulfo's prose is sprinkled with regional expressions and concrete rural images that illuminate the bleak Jaliscan landscape and reflect the tragic lives of his protagonists. Although the interior monologue of "Es que somos muy pobres" reproduces the disjointed thought patterns and rambling syntax of a bewildered adolescent, on closer examination it reveals a high degree of stylization for poetic effect, relying on abrupt temporal dislocations, repetitions with variation, and the deft use of conjunctions to render the impression of spontaneity and vitality. The end result is a dynamic, but carefully measured portrait of dramatic human proportions that transcends the limits of rural Mexico.

The same year that Rulfo's story appeared, Paraguay's best living writer, Augusto Roa Bastos (1918–   ), published "La excavación" (1953; "The Excavation"). An ingenious melange of social protest and symbolism, "La excavación" portrays a political prisoner, Perucho Rodi, who many years previously had fought in the Chaco War between Paraguay and Bolivia (1932–1935). While Rodi is digging an escape tunnel for his fellow prisoners and himself, the ground above him collapses, entombing him alive. As he frantically attempts to claw his way out, he loses consciousness, and just before he dies, relives an episode during the war when he and other Paraguayan soldiers dug a tunnel behind enemy lines and massacred an entire unit of Bolivians.

"La excavación" can be read on several different levels, the most obvious being that of social protest. In addition to the shocking prison conditions, Roa Bastos depicts the atrocities of war and alludes to the exploitation of Paraguayans and Bolivians by foreign economic powers. On a symbolic level, the story reveals possible influences of Borges, for whom Roa Bastos has expressed the highest esteem. The two tunnels resemble Borgesian labyrinths, the first leading Rodi to his death rather than freedom, and the second representing a conduit to the very center of his psyche, where he confronts his double in the form of the Bolivian soldier he had killed during the earlier massacre. Now alive and armed with a machine gun, the double shoots Rodi exactly as he had been shot by Rodi many years before.

An additional dimension of "La excavación" is provided by its mythical underpinnings, which not only illuminate its overall meaning but enhance its structural unity. Rodi emerges as the representative of an entire people struggling against oppression, but unlike the mythical hero, he is doomed to lose because of his own sins against his fellow man. His sins are magnified and thus linked metaphorically to those of mankind; moreover, in his nightmare of the Chaco War his Bolivian victims assume the appearance of his fellow prisoners who in the final lines of the story are massacred by their guards after being enticed to escape through the unlocked prison doors. Rodi, then, is both a hero and a traitor, one who must sacrifice his life for the cause of freedom because the evil he committed in his past lives on in the present. This dichotomy within the human personality, which Borges views as merely another of life's baffling phenomena, becomes a fundamental cause for Roa Bastos's pessimistic view of the human experience.

During the 1950s an outstanding group of young Peruvian writers gave new directions to the national literature, shifting their focus from rural to urban settings and establishing a balance between regional and universal themes. Although they continued to protest against social injustice, they also relied on technical innovations and stylistic artistry to dramatize the alienation increasingly characteristic of life in Peru's burgeoning capital. The leading representative of this generation is Julio Ramón Ribeyro (1929–   ), whose "Los gallinazos sin plumas" (1955; the Featherless Buzzards) has become a classic in Peruvian fiction. In this hair-raising tale, two young brothers living in a slum are obliged by their grandfather to collect garbage to fatten his pig, Pascual, which he plans to sell for a handsome profit. When the boys are unable to work for several days because of illness, their grandfather throws their pet dog into the pigsty to satisfy the voracious animal. In anger one of the youngsters strikes the old man, causing him to fall into the sty where he is attacked and presumably killed.

The theme of "Los gallinazos sin plumas" is effectively conveyed by marxist symbolism. The insatiable, monstrous Pascual represents the capitalistic system based on economic growth through exploitation; the grandfather emerges as the exploiter who nurtures the system for his own gain; and the boys (the "featherless buzzards") stand for the exploited, alienated proletariat that Marx encouraged to revolt against its oppressors.

The marxist ideology and the sordid, naturalistic events are embellished by poetic devices that enhance the story's esthetic value. The rhythmic repetition of images and the adroit use of foreshadowing techniques sustain suspense up to the climatic ending. When the omniscient narrator describes the city through the minds of the young boys, it assumes a mysterious, magical quality, at times even conveying a sense of adventure. At other times, however, the city exudes a foreboding of doom, as in the final lines when it is described as a monster opening its "gigantic jaws" to devour the terrified youngsters who are fleeing from their slum dwelling. Ribeyro's tale is also replete with irony, the most obvious example being the grandfather's destruction by the monster he himself created. In addition, this episode suggests that the rigid, uncompromising upper classes in and beyond Spanish America could bring about their own apocalyptic downfall.

Several years before the generation of the 1950s began to revitalize Peruvian fiction, a similar phenomenon had taken place in Puerto Rico. The island's so-called generation of 1940, which in reality emerged during the late 1940s and early 1950s, enriched Puerto Rico's picturesque, regionalistic literature with innovative techniques and popular linguistic patterns at the same time it set out to reaffirm the national identity of a people dominated politically, economically, and culturally by the United States. One of the leaders of this group is Pedro Juan Soto (1928–   ), whose "Garabatos" (1956; "Scribbles") typifies this short fiction. The story of a poor Puerto Rican family living in a New York tenement, "Garabatos" dramatizes two basic yet distinctly different themes: the extreme hardships suffered by the uprooted Puerto Rican immigrant to the United States mainland, and the alienation of the misunderstood artist. These two distinctly different themes underlie the binary opposition that gives dramatic tension and structural cohesion to Soto's tale. Amid the sordid reality of the family's desperate economic circumstances, Graciela makes disparaging references to what she considers the absurd artistic endeavors (scribbles) of her husband, Rosendo. The family's basement apartment reflects the Puerto Rican's position on the lowest rung of the social ladder, just as Rosendo's drawing on the bathroom wall—the only wall not covered with religious prints—demonstrates the subordinate role relegated to art in a poverty-ridden society.

The binary opposition shaping the story's structure also stems from the contrasting images of the filthy, snow-covered streets visible from the apartment window and the pristine Puerto Rican landscape Rosendo remembers from his youth. This dichotomy between ugly reality and romantic ideal is reinforced by the antithetical protagonists, Graciela, the practical, embittered realist, and Rosendo, the dreamer doomed to failure. When Graciela informs Rosendo that because of its sexual explicitness she has erased the picture he has drawn, his reaction is conveyed by the final sentence, which refers to the blank, grimy bathroom wall as "the wide and clear gravestone of [Rosendo's] dreams." This striking metaphor compresses the story's two principal themes into a single image, unifying structural design and underscoring meaning.

Like Pedro Juan Soto, Puerto Rico's best known contemporary writer René Marqués (1919–1979) belongs to the politically active Puerto Rican generation of 1940. An outspoken advocate of Puerto Rican independence from the United States, Marqués wrote many fine stories that reveal his preoccupation with the island's political and cultural destiny as well as his existential anguish over the passing of time and the individual's futile search for identity. "Purificación en la calle de Cristo" (1960; "Purification on Cristo Street") portrays three elderly upper-class Puerto Rican sisters whose lives reflect the vicissitudes of the island's history since the latter part of the nineteenth century. In the minds of Inés and Amelia, the recent demise of Hortensia evokes memories of the past that revive their guilt complexes, Inés's for informing Hortensia of her fiancé's love affair with another woman, and Amelia's for also being in love with Hortensia's fiancé. When she heard of the affair, Hortensia incarcerated herself and her younger sisters in the family mansion, where they lived in steadily worsening financial straits, refusing to recognize the changes that took place in their native land. In the final lines Inés and Amelia, hounded by American creditors, set the deteriorating mansion on fire with themselves and their dead sister in it.

Marqués's use of the shifting indirect interior monologue is particularly effective in this story because it affords the characters the opportunity to express their preoccupations with the past, creating the impression that they have achieved their objective of stopping the flow of time. Inés's attempt to preserve the beauty of bygone days and thus expiate her guilt is symbolized by the family jewels she has kept hidden. In her fleeting imagination, an ugly water stain on the wall that takes the form of an isthmus between two continents links an unpleasant episode of the past (the loss of the family's country estate) with one in the present (Hortensia's death from cancer). The American military occupation and economic domination of the island provide additional motivation for the act of "purification," setting fire to the house. The sisters' guilt complexes become a metaphor of the collective guilt Marqués attributes to Puerto Rico, and the final dramatic scene alluded to in the title, the expression of his desire for a complete political and cultural renovation.

The most talented Spanish American writer of short fiction to appear on the literary scene since Borges is the Argentine Julio Cortázar (1914–   ), who is often compared to his more famous countryman. A major difference between the two is that Borges fabricates bookish tales based on literature and philosophy, whereas Cortázar excels at depicting poetic facets of humdrum, everyday life. Cortázar's works are characterized by generous doses of fantasy, but he has also been profoundly influenced by surrealism and the philosophy of the Absurd. One of his surrealistic masterpieces is "La noche boca arriba" (1956; "The Night Face Up"), the tale of a youth injured in a motorcycle accident as he speeds through a beautiful modern city, presumably in Mexico. While recovering after surgery, he dreams that he is a Motec Indian fleeing from the Aztecs who capture him and prepare to sacrifice him to their gods. His dream is frequently interrupted, however, by brief moments of awareness of his hospital surroundings. In the nightmarish climax, he finds himself on the steps of a pyramid waiting to be sacrificed when suddenly he realizes that dream and reality have been reversed.

The fluctuations between reality and dream generate abrupt changes in mood that are intensified by the emotionally charged atmosphere and sensual imagery of both the hospital and the exotic Mexican setting. The feverish protagonist imagines that between the initial impact of his accident and the moment when he was picked up from the pavement he sank into a black pit of nothingness for what seemed an eternity. This temporal dislocation is repeated throughout the story as he is wrenched again and again from the comfort of his hospital bed into the horror of his nightmare. Still, numerous parallels between his conscious and unconscious states create a unifying, reflecting-mirror structure that foreshadows the surrealistic denouement. Thus the stretcher on which he is placed prior to his operation can be linked to his sensation of being carried face-up through a passageway of the pyramid; the lights and medicinal odors of the hospital reappear as Aztec torches and the cloying smells of war; the pulley holding his broken arm immobile is repeated in the ropes binding him to a stone slab; and his surgery emerges as a prelude to his sacrifice by a knife-wielding Indian priest.

In many of his works, Cortázar searches for the surrealist absolute, that intermediate gray zone between reality and dream where contradictions unite and antinomies are abolished. In "La noche boca arriba" he goes a step further, transforming objective reality into an insane dream and the terrible nightmare of Aztec savagery into reality, but he nevertheless accomplishes something akin to the surrealists' goal. The final esthetically charged lines of the story jolt the reader into a keen awareness of the precarious balance between the rational consciousness and the unconscious, an awareness that undermines faith in reason and creates an expanded, multidimensional surreality.

Another of Cortázar's masterpieces is "Las babas del diablo" (1958; "Blow-up"), on which Michelangelo Antonioni based his famous experimental film Blow-up (1966). the protagonist of this story is Robert Michel, a French-Chilean translator and amateur photographer who takes a snapshot of a woman and a boy on the Isle Saint-Louis in Paris, surmising that what he has witnessed is the woman's attempted seduction of her young companion. Immediately thereafter Michel is confronted by the hostile woman and a man who approaches from a car parked nearby. Meanwhile the boy has taken flight. Several days later Michel enlarges the snapshot and once again finds himself drawn into the scene, which takes on new meaning. To his horror, he now realizes that the agent of seduction was not the woman but the man. Thus in his imagination he relives the episode of the photograph, this time focusing his camera on the man and again giving the boy the opportunity to escape.

"Las babas del diablo" is the type of tale that lends itself to various interpretations, but it is primarily an example of self-conscious metafiction, that is, a story about writing a story. In the opening lines, the narrator alludes to his predicament over how to relate the events he has witnessed, and throughout his story he alludes to the clouds drifting across the sky, symbols of an evanescent reality neither film nor words can capture. The analogies between the art of photography and the art of fiction serve to illuminate the metafictional theme; the camera and the typewriter are referred to as lifeless tools manipulated by the photographer and the writer as means of capturing a rigid fragment of fleeting reality by way of static images and words. If the photograph is good (and we are told that this one is), it can act like an explosion on the viewer, disclosing a dynamic, open-ended reality, just as the artistically conceived story often points to something beyond itself. Michel's enlargement takes on a life of its own, revealing a new element in the drama he saw. Similarly, his story acquires new dimensions as he reworks it and becomes emotionally involved with his three characters. Like "La noche boca arriba," which transforms reality into a surrealist nightmare, "Las babas del diablo" subverts the reality of the original snapshot, the enlargement of which becomes a metaphor of a creative process.

"Las babas del diablo" recalls "El Aleph," both of which dramatize the frustrations involved in the art of writing fiction. Borges resolves the problem of depicting a simultaneous vision (the Aleph) in linear language by creating a symbolic, intuitively apprehended Aleph (Beatriz) that defies the erosion of time. Cortázar requires the reader's active participation in the re-creation of his story, obliging him to grasp intuitively the metafictional implications of the enlarged snapshot.

Among the numerous satirical salvos directed against American imperialism by Latin American writers is "Mr. Taylor" (1959), by Augusto Monterroso (1921–   ), who, although born in Guatemala, has resided in Mexico since 1944. An American living with a tribe of primitive Indians in the Amazon region of South America, Mr. Taylor founds a highly lucrative business with his uncle, Mr. Ralston, exporting shrunken heads to be sold as artifacts in the United States. When the supply of heads provided by natural deaths fails to meet the increasing demand, tribal doctors are encouraged to let their patients die, the death sentence is imposed for minor crimes, and wars are declared against all neighboring tribes. Still the supply remains insufficient. The story ends with the arrival in Mr. Ralston's New York office of a package from South America containing the protagonist's shrunken head.

The symbolism of Monterroso's tale is obvious. Taylor's export business represents the gringos' economic exploitation of Latin America, whose leaders are frequently only too willing to assist in the plunder of the nations they govern. In the manner of Jonathan Swift, the accumulation of hair-raising absurdities emerges as the principal structuring device of the story, which like all satire, is also laced with irony. Thus Mr. Taylor is repeatedly referred to as a man of vast culture and artistic sensitivity, although it is he who advises the president to declare war on the neighboring tribes just to assure his own continued prosperity. In view of the story's climactic ending, moreover, it is ironic that on his arrival in South America, Mr. Taylor is known among the Indians as "the poor *gringo*."

Innovative Forms and the Boom

During the 1960s the short story as a genre continued the major trends of the preceding decade, reflecting the political realities as well as the philosophical and esthetic preoccupations of a wide variety of writers. Although during this decade of the much-touted Boom the novel tended to overshadow short fiction, the short story of the 1960s reached heights of quality and originality that remain unsurpassed to the present. A major achievement of the year 1960 is "Paseo" ("The Walk") by José Donoso (1925–), Chile's most prestigious man of letters. In this deceptively simple tale Donoso uses Jungian psychology and an ironically detached narrator to dramatize the dichotomy between the rational and instinctual spheres of the human psyche. The protagonist is a straitlaced spinster named Matilde who supervises the household of her brothers, all successful lawyers. The strictly observed routine of their existence is disrupted when a white mongrel bitch follows Matilde home from church and little by little wins her affection. One night she takes the dog for a walk and never returns.

At the beginning of the story Matilde is presented as a rationally oriented person, whose rigid sense of order and inability to show affection indicate suppression of the instinctual side of her psyche, the side that, according to Jung, must be recognized and nurtured so that one can achieve a complete personality. The mongrel bitch represents Matilde's shadow, the repressed archetype of her unconscious that takes gradual possession of her, causing her daily routine to crumble, restoring her vitality, and inviting her to participate in life's unknown adventures. When it first attaches itself to her, it is a filthy, ailing stray, abhorrent to her strict sense of cleanliness and order. After she had bathed, fed, and restored it to health, symbolizing the recognition and nurturing of her shadow, the dog not only becomes an integral part of her consciousness but even dominates her conduct and brings about her mysterious disappearance.

The story's irony stems from its point of view; the narrator is Matilde's nephew, now a middle-aged man, who recalls the events as he witnessed them when he was a child. This narrative distance, together with the child's horror over Matilde's unknown fate, strikes an ironic chord because the implied man behind the stodgy, middle-aged persona probably views her disappearance as a liberation from a life worse than death.

"Paseo" is replete with symbols and leitmotivs that reinforce its major theme and unify its structure. The boat sirens and city lights represent the irrational unconscious, and the nightly, ritualistic billiard games, the rigid routine dominating the lives of the excessively rationalistic characters. The story is symmetrically framed by the thick library doors, which muffle voices from within and thus symbolize the lack of communication in the narrator's boyhood home. Donoso's portrait of Matilde shatters the concept of the unified personality and, like much contemporary fiction, makes irony and ambiguity major esthetic ingredients.

"En el gran Ecbo" (1960; "At the Great 'Ecbo'"), by Cuba's Guillermo Cabrera Infante (1929–   ) dramatizes another psychological situation fraught with ambiguity. In this tale, a young middle-class Cuban couple attends a religious ceremony of blacks honoring their dead and worshiping their god of purity. During the ceremony an old black woman speaks briefly to the young lady, who immediately thereafter terminates her relationship with her male companion.

Cabrera Infante's technique is reminiscent of Hemingway's, namely, his laconic dialogues, his sparse descriptions of surface reality, and his flat, deadpan tone. He also effectively uses the technique of suspended coherence, reversing normal cause and effect relationships to create suspense. Thus we are told that the young lady is obsessed by death and feelings of remorse before we learn why; allusions are made to photographs the man has shown her that subsequently turn out to be (we assume) of his wife and child; and although we remain in doubt about why she terminates the relationship, we surmise that the ceremony, and especially her conversation with the old black woman, externalize her feelings of guilt for living in sin with a married man.

The story owes its tautness to two sets of opposites: the antithetical natures of the couple and the gulf between the white middle-class and black cultures in Cuba. The man is rationalistic and arrogant, viewing the religious ceremony as an exotic after-lunch diversion, while his companion emerges as a sensitive, intuitive individual deeply moved by the fervor of the participants. The schism between cultures comes to light through the structure of the story, the first part of which presents the slightly bored, bourgeois couple dining in a restaurant during a rainstorm, and the second, the magic-charged atmosphere of the ceremony, climaxing with the enigmatic episode of the black woman. Published in the same year, "Paseo" and "En el gran Ecbo" have much in common. Both are skillfully executed psychological portraits, both are full of ambiguity, and both depict the vulnerability of the upper middle class, which in Donoso's tale is threatened by the Jungian unconscious and in Cabrera Infante's by the more instinctual lower classes.

The artist's role in society becomes a major theme of "La prodigiosa tarde de Baltazar" (1962; "Baltazar's Marvelous Afternoon"), by Colombia's leading man of letters, Gabriel García Márquez (1928–   ). Baltazar is a thirty-year-old carpenter who makes an elaborate bird cage for the son of the town's most affluent citizen, José Montiel. The latter's refusal to pay for the cage and Baltazar's generous gesture toward the boy lead to the story's climax and denouement.

As the central motif, the cage symbolizes artistic creativity and illuminates the conflict between the ideal realm of imagination and the concrete world of reality. Baltazar represents the prototype of the artist whose generous, childlike nature stands in sharp contrast to the selfish, belligerent Montiel. Imagination and sordid reality also clash in the final episode, which portrays the inebriated, penniless Baltazar sprawled out on the street, vaguely aware that someone is stealing his shoes, but unwilling to abandon the happiest dream of his life.

In marxist terms, Montiel may be viewed as the bourgeois capitalist interested only in the accumulation of wealth, whereas the other citizens of the town, all of whom resent his power, represent the proletariat. Also illustrated is the marxist contention that in a capitalist society art becomes a commodity, an alien, antagonistic force devoid of its former sacredness. Baltazar, of course, does not see his art in this light, nor, at the beginning of the story, do his friends. Montiel's reference to the cage as a trinket that Baltazar should sell to whoever will buy it typifies the bourgeois attitude toward artistic endeavor that Marx deplored. When Baltazar arrives at the pool hall, his friends have lost all interest in his creation, seeing it only in terms of the money he has been able to extract from the niggardly Montiel.

The confrontation between Baltazar and Montiel also exemplifies the dialectic method of presentation that Marx alludes to in his literary criticism. Thus dramatic movement is generated by polarized characteristics such as idealism/materialism, sensitivity/insensitivity, poverty/wealth, generosity/avarice, and kindness/cruelty. For Baltazar, the artist, the synthesis resulting from his confrontation with Montiel may be a moral victory, but it is gained only through economic loss and alienation from a society that judges art only in terms of monetary value.

Magical realism is a term critics of Spanish American literature have bandied about for more than twenty-five years, but because it has yet to be defined precisely and universally, some critics would prefer not to use or even recognize the term.[4] Still, it would be impossible in any survey discussion of recent Spanish American fiction to ignore this literary mode about which so much has been said. Basically, magical realism attempts to penetrate objective reality and to reveal the mysterious and poetic qualities underlying the daily lives of a community or people. With a few notable exceptions, it is found primarily in countries with large Indian or black populations, that is, wherever European civilization is only a veneer superimposed on hidden layers of primitive cultures.

A fascinating example of magical realism is "La culpa es de los tlaxcaltecas" (1964; "It's All the Fault of the Tlaxcaltecas") by Elena Garro (1920–   ) of Mexico. The title alludes to the conquest of Mexico, when the Tlaxcaltecas aided Cortés in his struggle against their enemies, the Aztecs, thus betraying their Indian heritage. The story's protagonist is an upper middle-class white woman who feels that she too has betrayed her heritage because she believes that in a previous existence she was the wife of an Aztec warrior fighting against the Spanish conquerors. When her dual role becomes unbearable, she renounces the modern world and disappears into the mythical past.

Like most magically real fiction, Garro's tale includes many commonplace details of contemporary Spanish American life. In addition, the protagonist's monotonous existence is constantly interrupted by scenes of the battle for the Aztec capital, which she witnesses while her husband fights to repel the foreign invader. Particularly impressive are the poetic devices and structural techniques used to distort time and render the fantastic plot almost believable. Garro's style is highly sensual and evocative, relying heavily on mysterious lighting effects, sounds, and olfactory images designed to blur the reader's perceptions and preface the abrupt flashbacks into remote history. Ingeniously interwoven dialogues frequently accompany these temporal dislocations, replacing narration by the omniscient author and enhancing the overall impression of two true-to-life dramas existing simultaneously. The juxtaposition of the realistic present and the mythical past not only expands esthetic dimensions, but conveys the story's principal theme, that ancient myths still permeate twentieth-century Mexican life, undermining logic and altering individual destinies.

The dehumanization of man in a technological society has been treated by numerous Spanish American writers, but none has developed this theme with more artistry and humor than the popular Argentine satirist Marco Denevi (1922–   ). His fable "La mariposa" (1965; The Butterfly) describes a colony of ants whose food scientists discover how to manufacture synthetically, thus removing the ants' dependence on nature. Immersed in their artifical realm governed by the laws of technology, they are sealed off in the anthill and soon forget about the outside world. Generations later an ant somehow makes his way through a forgotten exit and discovers the marvels of nature. Dazzled and ecstatic, he returns to inform his fellow ants, but when he reappears before them transformed into a beautiful butterfly, they think he is a monster and kill him.

"La mariposa" satirizes modern man's lack of human qualities and separation from nature as well as his loss of freedom and creativity. The butterfly symbolizes the misunderstood artist whose talent and spontaneity are stifled by a society in which the individual is subordinated to the machine. Denevi's style is simple and direct, making his message unmistakably clear, lacing his narration with both technical jargon and poetic images to underscore the barriers between technology and art. The scientifically oriented ants' conviction that their hermetic domicile represents the real world is reminiscent of Borges's "Tlön, Uqbar, Orbis Tertius," in which a well-ordered, but imaginary planet is also embraced as reality. Denevi's irony is enhanced by the dialectic opposites underlying his story's structural framework, examples of which include the progressive aspect of the ants' social organization, their "antiprogressive" denial of history, the roving ant's discovery of poetic beauty in the real world, and the wanton murder of the butterfly.

Salvador Elizondo (1932–   ) is another Mexican writer whose works, like those of Juan José Arreola, share many characteristics with Borges's. Elizondo similarly uses philosophical ideas to create fiction, and like his two elder colleagues, looks beyond Latin America for much of his inspiration. "La historia según Pao Cheng" (1966; History According to Pao Cheng) emerges as an ingenious spoof of Borges's metaphysical *ficciones,* its themes of circular and philosophical idealism serving as the warp and woof of its content. Pao Cheng is an ancient Chinese philosopher who views history as a repetitive series of events. One day he imagines himself walking through a foreign city of the future where he discovers a man writing a story about him, Pao Cheng, who imagines that he (Pao Cheng) is in a city of the future where he (Pao Cheng) discovers a man writing a story, et cetera. Suddenly the author of the story about Pao Cheng realizes that he is no more than a memory of Pao Cheng in his own story, and that if Pao Cheng forgets him, he will die. So the author of the story of Pao Cheng finds himself condemned for eternity to continue writing the story of Pao Cheng because if Pao Cheng is forgotten, the author, who is only a memory of Pao Cheng, will disappear.

From the preceding summary, the importance of circular time in Elizondo's story is clearly evident. Even more important is his use of idealism as a basis for plot. The author of the story of Pao Cheng, like the magus of Borges's "Las ruinas circulares," is horrified to learn that he exists only in somebody else's mind. What makes Elizondo's tale a spoof of Borges's metaphysical work, however, is not only his treatment of time and idealism, but the fact that he (Elizondo) carries idealism a step beyond what Borges had done. In "Las ruinas circulares," for example, the magus (Borges's creation) concludes that he (the magus), like the man he has dreamed, is no more than an abstract idea in the mind of another. In Elizondo's tale, Pao Cheng (Elizondo's creation) exists in the imagination of another (like Borges's magus at the end of "Las ruinas circulares"), but the other is Pao Cheng's fictitious creation and this fictitious creation realizes that he exists only in his creator's (Pao Cheng's) mind. Thus, to continue to exist he must keep his creator (Pao Cheng) alive in his (the author's) mind by forever writing his story about Pao Cheng.

When a fictitious character in another fictitious character's imagination realizes that his existence depends on the continuation of the first character's imaginary existence, it would seem that the laws of idealism have been carried to absurdity. Borges himself would probably applaud Elizondo's playful endeavor because, like Borges's works, it dissolves objective reality and thrusts the reader into a fictitious, cerebral world not unlike the realm of history.

Although very different from Elizondo's philosophical abstractions, Julio Cortázar's "Autopista del sur" (1966; "The Southern Thruway") also dramatizes an absurd situation, namely, a massive traffic jam that begins on a Sunday afternoon in August and lasts until the following spring. The travelers on the six-lane double highway leading to Paris gradually form communes consisting of the cars in their immediate vicinity, and endeavor to deal with everyday problems such as procurement of food and water, treatment of the sick, and the inevitable friction between individuals and communes. The leading chracter is an engineer driving a Peugeot 404 who befriends a girl in a Dauphine. In the final lines of the story the bottleneck is finally eliminated and the cars speed toward Paris.

At the start of the traffic jam the travelers find themselves faced with circumstances entirely beyond their control, their movements toward their respective goals halted and their schedules totally disrupted. Their confrontation with this chaotic situation, which recalls Camus's definition of the Absurd, induces them to organize a kind of world in microcosm, a reflection of the mores and institutions men have lived by for generations. Thus their communes restore a semblance of order to their lives, but from Cortázar's point of view it is an order achieved through mindless routine, which the travelers accept passively without ever rousing themselves to ask "Why?" When the traffic jam finally dissolves, the engineer finds that he longs for the daily rituals of the past few months. In the final lines of the story he and the others are once again encapsulated in their metal cages, racing through the night to begin anew, one assumes, a routine existence as meaningless and absurd as the one from which they have just been freed.

"Autopista del sur" condemns today's emphasis on the mechanization that crushes individual identities and weakens human bonds. Thus the characters' names are usurped by those of their automobiles, and the engineer, who has fallen in love with the girl in the Dauphine and even fathered her unborn child, loses her, presumably forever, when their cars become separated in the rush toward Paris. For Cortázar, rituals and routine represent compulsive attempts to ward off the solitude and chaos that threaten the individual in a world he can neither understand nor control. "Autopista del sur" and Arreola's "El guardagujas" have much in common, both dramatizing human experience symbolized by the journey. A major difference is that Arreola's traveler-protagonist ultimately boards the train, having been fully apprised of life's absurdity, whereas Cortázar's travelers move from one episode to another without ever confronting the existential reality of the modern world.

The death of the Argentine communist guerrilla Che Guevara in Bolivia in 1967 is the subject of one of Bolivia's finest contemporary short stories, "La emboscada" (1967; The Ambush) by Adolfo Caceres Romero (1937–   ). A complex montage of narrative fragments, this ingeniously structured tale relates an incident that occurs immediately after Che Guevara's body is found by his last surviving comrade, who is referred to as "the man." When the latter enters a hut in search of food, he is captured by deserters from Guevara's guerrilla band and hanged from a nearby tree. Meanwhile a young Bolivian army captain and his men surround the hut, but they are killed in an ambush by the deserters.

One of the few innovators in Bolivian fiction during the 1960s, Caceres Romero relates a disjointed chain of events by constantly shifting the point of view from the man to the captain to the omniscient narrator, all of whom inject snatches of dialogue into their fragments of the story. This technique facilitates the narrative movement from exterior to interior planes of action, from present to past or future tense, and from real to imaginary occurrences. For example, as he dissects Che Guevara's body to keep it from falling into enemy hands, the man recalls the bloody ambush in which his leader died. During this same skirmish the captain's mind flashes back to an incident in his past of shooting at a revolving lantern (la calesita) in a carnival. In anticipation of his victorious return to his base of operations, he imagines interviews with newsmen, eulogies from his superiors, and a promotion to the rank of major as a reward for his bravery.

Numerous leitmotivs link these episodes and give a more coherent pattern to the story's literary texture. The guerrilla capitana waving a white handkerchief during the ambush is evoked by both the man and the captain; as are barking dogs that pursue the guerrillas, discover the hanged man, and carry off Che Guevara's bones. Both the man and the captain catch sight of the river swollen with bloodstained bodies and the vultures hovering above. The captain's happy memory of the revolving carnival lantern stands out in ironic contrast to the tragic situation he first creates and to which he finally falls victim.

"La emboscada" is a fictitious account of Che Guevara's death and its aftermath; historic documents have revealed that in reality he was captured by the Bolivian army and executed the following day. Caceres Romero's tale does, however, exude the true-to-life aura of pessimism the Argentine revolutionary's fate left among Latin American artists and intellectuals.

As might be expected, Cuba's literary generation of 1960 has probed various aspects of Fidel Castro's revolution. Although magical realism and fantasy characterize the works of some of these young, imaginative writers, the most original of the group, Norberto Fuentes (1943–   ), seems to have been inspired primarily by the neorealistic traditions of Hemingway and Rulfo. "El capitán Descalzo" (1968; "Captain Descalzo") is one of Fuentes's stories that dramatize the counterinsurgency campaign undertaken by the Cuban government between 1960 and 1966. A former captain in the revolutionary forces, Descalzo has returned to his plot of land from which he earns a precarious living for himself and his children. When an insurgent fleeing from the militia accosts Descalzo in a field he has been plowing, Descalzo kills him with a machete. He then returns to his house and chats with the militia commander before telling him where the body is to be found.

Fuentes's narrative technique is particularly reminiscent of Hemingway's, the language intense, unadorned, and concise, and the point of view that of the direct observer (as opposed to the ominiscient narrator), who, like a movie camera, limits the fictional material to action, dialogue, and surface reality. His style is elliptical, concentrating on nouns and verbs rather than adjectives to stimulate the reader's imagination, heighten suspense, and accelerate the flow of events. The structural pattern is anticipated by the initial contrast between Descalzo's plowed land and the tropical jungle bordering it. The ensuing scene presents the two antagonists, Descalzo and the insurgent, the former with his well-cared-for machete and the latter with his rusty Luger, a symbol of Cuba's rejected past. After killing the insurgent, Descalzo reveals in his conversation with the militia commander that unlike other revolutionary officers who have profited handsomely from their role in the fighting, he is a simple, rustic man who can tolerate neither shoes on his feet nor life in the city (descalzo is the Spanish word for barefoot). Ultimately his calm revelation of the terrible deed he has just committed likens him to an epic hero or an Old Testament patriarch whose actions transcend the specific time and place in which they occur. Descalzo's brutality also underscores the firm resolve of a nation recently reborn to achieve its revolutionary goals.

In the mid-1960s the Mexican literary scene was profoundly altered by a movement known as la onda, (the wave) and composed of young irreverent writers. Closely related to the worldwide student rebellion of this period, *la onda* reflected the nonconformity of youth and its rejection of traditional bourgeois values. One of the leaders of this group was José Agustín (1944–   ), whose "Cuál es la onda" (1968; "What's Cool") more than any other piece of short fiction typifies this movement. The protagonists are a young drummer, Oliveira, and a girl named Requelle, who initiates their friendship at a dance. They spend the night in a series of sleazy hotels, mocking virtually every aspect of the establishment in the iconoclastic, juvenile vernacular that emerges as both the medium and the message of the story.

Agustín's choice of the name Oliveira suggests the possible influence of Cortázar, whose famous novel *Rayuela* (1963) presents a protagonist of the same name. Somewhat like Cortázar, Agustín creates a spontaneous language consisting of colloquial words, puns, and popular foreign phrases, all of which represent a reaction to the rigid linguistic patterns as well as to the out-moded institutions of the status quo. He also reveals the strong influence of rock music groups such as the Beatles and the Rolling Stones, whose rhythms he re-creates in the humorous banter of his two youthful characters. Occasionally, he shifts the narrative perspective, abruptly injecting an offhand, and at times insulting, remark to the reader or an amusing authorial comment on the creative process. The ironic tone resulting from this technique becomes a major unifying element and also tends to make the reader laugh at, rather than identify with, the ludicrous antics of the couple.

There are several episodes that illustrate the satirical nature of the story, and exchanges in which Augustín pokes fun at government propaganda, Mexico's lagging technology, and the hypocritical attitude of the Latin macho toward sex. In spite of the rebellious tone conveyed by the language and the sexual liberation implicit in the plot, the union of the protagonists is never consummated, and the following morning, though lacking the necessary legal papers, they unsuccessfully attempt to bribe a judge to marry them. Furthermore, in an unguarded moment of self-revelation, Oliveira confesses that he is a middle-class prude at heart. It would seem, then, that Agustín's satire of middle-class Mexican society may also represent a parody of young rebels, whose rejection of tradition is more palaver than substance and whose future is destined to evolve like that of their elders once the crisis of youth has passed. Agustín's fertile imagination and linguistic agility illustrated in works such as "Cuál es la onda" made him the enfant terrible of Mexican letters during the 1960s. Today, a decade and a half later, he has become one of Mexico's leading intellectuals.

Although science fiction in Spanish America has not enjoyed the success it has had in the United States, it has produced some highly imaginative, artistically conceived works. One of these is "Una cuerda de nylón y oro" (1969; A Rope of Nylon and Gold) by the Salvadoran Alvaro Menéndez Leal (also known as Alvaro Menén Desleal, (1931–   ). The first-person narrator of this tale is an American as-tronaut who leaps from this spaceship for a walk in space, but instead of completing the tasks he has been trained to perform, he cuts the cord attached to his capsule and continues to orbit the earth as a free agent. After an unspecified length of time, he witnesses a nuclear war that destroys the entire planet below and submerges it into darkness.

Menéndez Leal's technical jargon, sharp visual imagery, and accurate references to the space race in 1965, the year the action occurs, lend credibility to his story, the irony of which emerges as a major literary ingredient. Feeling supremely free and happy for having severed all contact with his fellow men, the narrator-protagonist is able to view human foibles, political intrigues, and natural disasters with complete detachment, thus underscoring the absurdity of the world he has left behind. The juxtaposition of unrelated information ("There was a presi-dent named Johnson, and my wife was sleeping with Sam Wilson") further illustrates the ironic perspective, a perspective the reader even-tually comes to share. Also significant is the fact that most of the events seen from afar place the United States in a bad light, the nefarious activities of the Ku Klux Klan and the war in Vietnam serving as prime examples. In this science fiction tale fraught with political overtones, the nation responsible for the imagined nuclear holocaust is clearly identifiable.

Myth, Fantasy, and Reality: 1970s

The decade of the 1970s, while not lacking in short fiction of high quality, produced fewer new, innovative writers than the 1960s. Al-though one can only speculate on the reasons for this phenomenon, the end of the Boom in the novel, the slackening of student activism, and the relative political tranquility (except for Chile and Nicaragua) are possible explanations. Also significant is the gradually deteriorating economic situation of the 1970s, which made publishing increasingly difficult for all but the well-established authors.

In 1970, after seventeen years of silence in the genre of short fiction, Borges published *El informe de Brodie* (*Doctor Brodie's Report*), a collection of stories that, unlike his complex metaphysical stories of the 1940s, is written, as the author himself has stated, in the straightforward style of the young Rudyard Kipling. The protagonist of "El evangelio según Marcos" (1970; "The Gospel According to Mark"), one of Borges's own favorites, is a thirty-three-year-old medical student named Baltasar Espinosa who is spending the summer on his cousin's ranch. While the latter is in Buenos Aires on business, a severe rainstorm causes a flood, isolating Espinosa, together with the foreman Gutre, and Gutre's son and daughter. Every night after dinner Espinosa reads to his three illiterate companions a portion of the Gospel according to St. Mark, which seems to fascinate them. One day Gutre asks Espinosa if Christ allowed himself to be crucified for the sake of all men, and although he is a free thinker, Espinosa feels obliged to answer in the affirmative. The story ends as the Gutres prepare to crucify Espinosa.

"El evangelio según Marcos" dramatizes two of Borges's favorite themes: circular time and the perpetually recurring human experience. Baltasar Espinosa emerges as a modern Christ figure, his Christian name recalling one of the three Magi and his surname ("thorn" in English), Christ's crown of thorns. His age, his kindly nature, and his outstanding ability as an orator represent additional characteristics of the Christian savior, while the pet lamb he cures brings to mind the significant amount of Christian symbolism involving lambs, including the sacrificial lamb that Espinosa himself will become. Espinosa's dream of the flood and the construction of the Ark foreshadow his act of redemption for the Gutres.

The allusions to the *Odyssey* and the Bible, the two stories men have always told and retold, have a direct bearing on the lives of the Gutres. Indeed, the history of the family is a kind of odyssey, since they had abandoned a civilized country (Scotland) for a remote, barbarous land where they lost their religion, forgot their native tongue, and regressed to ignorance and superstition. For them, the crucifixion represents a metaphoric return, a means of redemption and regeneration, for by sacrificing their redeemer they will supposedly assume his virtues.

Borges's reinterpretation of biblical myth suggests that although specific circumstances change, archetypal situations reflecting the essence of human behavior will be repeated ad infinitum. The climax of this tale, which occurs when Espinosa catches sight of the cross the Gutres have erected, is enhanced by the weeping of Gutre's daughter (a symbolic Mary Magdalene) and the song of a goldfinch (a symbol of the Passion of Christ). The surprise ending is also an example of what Borges has called the "esthetic reality," a kind of hovering, vertiginous moment of apprehension in which an inexpressible reality is intuited.

Very different from Borges's reworking of biblical myth is a subtle psychological portrait entitled "Biografía" (1971; Biography) by the Uruguayan Carlos Martínez Moreno (1917–   ). The protagonist is a recently deceased, middle-aged government employee, Manfredo, whose life is depicted through the mind of his wife Elena. Because of his good looks, Manfredo also worked as a model for cigarette advertisements that appeared in the most widely read newspapers and magazines. Just when his friend and photographer, Julio, was promising him better contracts with beer and whiskey companies, Manfredo fell ill with a brain tumor and died.

Elena's memories of her husband are evoked by photographs of him in various settings such as yachts, well-manicured gardens, luxurious restaurants, and football stadiums. He was always elegantly dressed and accompanied by beautiful women whom Elena envies because she herself has become fat. Elena also contrasts the photographs of her husband with their drab daily life together, which she attributes to his total lack of ambition in the government bureaucracy and to the meager sums Julio paid him. Manfredo's lingering death and Julio's indifference to the tragedy represent additional fragments of the past generating the story's overall meaning. The final lines are particularly illuminating. As Elena gazes at a photograph of Manfredo listening sympathetically to what a young lady is saying to him, she sees his entire biography clearly written on his face, a biography consisting of his attentiveness to the needs of others.

"Biografía" is not so much the story of a man's life as it is the portrait of his lonely widow. Elena, however, is not drawn explicitly through physical descriptions or psychological analyses; rather, she is artistically implied through a montage of evocative photographs of her husband whose synthetic, make-believe identity has become more palpably real to her than the man she subconsciously prefers to forget. The deftly manipulated direct and indirect interior monologues reinforce her feelings of alienation and thus reflect the story's dominant theme.

A type of humor heretofore unseen in this study is that of a young Argentine writer, Fernando Sorrentino (1942–   ), whose tale entitled "La pestilente historia de Antulín" (1972; "the Fetid Tale of Antulín")[5] is likely to elicit guffaws from most readers. The first-person narrator is a timid, meticulous occupant of a boarding house where Antulín, a slovenly, uncouth butcher, also makes his home. The narrator despises Antulín primarily because he must share the bathroom with this filthy, foul-smelling creature, who hangs his unwashed socks on the towel rack and has a copious bowel movement every morning at five o'clock, obliging the narrator to get up an hour before him to use the bathroom. After three frustrated attempts to kill his oafish enemy (by electrocution, fire, and gas), the narrator, although still seething with hate, is forced to abandon his efforts for revenge.

"La pestilente historia de Antulín" emerges as an exceptionally fine example of the grotesque, the purpose of which is to create tension in the reader's mind through the clash between the comic and an incompatible element such as disgust or horror. The reader's reaction to this unresolved incongruity can range from civilized repugnance to barbarous glee over the flouting of taboos, but the response is always emotional, never intellectual. Antulín's bathroom antics are particularly grotesque, as comedy is combined with scatology to produce predictable reader reactions. Additional examples of the grotesque are the narrator's attempts to murder the obnoxious Antulín, whose acute suffering from electric shock and burns as described is both horrible and hilarious.

The story's witty, artfully conceived style contributes much to its rollicking humor. The initial passages, for example, describe events in direct, realistic detail, but little by little pungent visual and olfactory images, hyperbolic distortions, and kafkaesque dream sequences create the absurd atmosphere that ultimately prevails. A unifying leitmotiv, repeated from beginning to end, is the narrator's obsessive reminder that he hates Antulín. His tone, moreover, oscillates between euphoric elation (when he thinks he has succeeded in murdering Antulín) and despair (when he realizes the lout has survived), a device that intensifies the reader's involvement in the ludicrous chain of events. The smoldering tension between the narrator and his nemesis is outwardly resolved when Antulín marries the landlady and becomes the overbearing owner of the boarding house. Antulín's triumph is also conveyed by the title of the story's final segment, "Olor constante más allá de la muerte" (Constant Odor beyond Death), a parody of Francisco Quevedo's sonnet, "Amor constante más allá de la muerte" (Constant Love beyond

Death), and García Márquez's tale, "Muerte constante más allá del amor" (Constant Death beyond Love).

As is obvious from the examples cited, the Mexican literary movement known as *la onda* consists of young, irreverent writers with a predilection for using juvenile slang and popular art forms to depict rebellious middle-class youths in the Mexican capital. Another tendency in recent Mexican letters is based on the concept of *escritura* ("writing"), that emphasizes universal themes as well as the subtle use of language and structure for poetic effect. A leading practitioner of *escritura* is José Emilio Pacheco (1939–   ), whose "La fiesta brava" (1972; The Fierce Sport of Bullfighting) constitutes a fine example of metafiction. The first part of this complex work consists of a story of the same title about an American army captain named Keller who commits atrocities in Vietnam and after having been discharged from the army, comes to Mexico as a tourist. While visiting the National Museum of Anthropology, he becomes fascinated with a statue of the earth goddess Coatlicue; the result is his nightmarish return to Mexico's remote past and his sacrifice to the Aztec sun god. The second portion of Pacheco's tale concerns the author of "La fiesta brava," Andrés Quintana, who submits his story to a *gringo* editor named Mr. Hardwick and later that same evening meets a fate similar to Keller's.

"La fiesta brava" (Pacheco's tale) evolves its meaning and esthetic unity through a series of parallels and contrasts that transcend the cultural and geographical borders of its immediate setting. The American presence in Vietnam is linked to American imperialism in Mexico when, just before he is sacrificed, Keller confuses his Aztec captors with his Vietnamese victims. In the second part of the story Mr. Hardwick, who not only edits the Mexican journal but also disburses the funds necessary for its existence, becomes an agent of cultural imperialism when he rejects Andrés's writing because of its anti-Yankee tone. For his literary efforts Andrés nevertheless receives one thousand of the six thousand pesos originally offered, a sum he feels obliged to accept because of need. Soon thereafter, however, he views the one thousand pesos as a form of Yankee domination, which triggers his feelings of self-contempt and anticipates the denouement. His final glimpse of Keller on the subway with three other passengers, and his own capture by three men as he leaves the subway, link his indentity to that of Keller, his inverted mirror image or antithetical double.

Before Andrés leaves Mr. Hardwick's office, his friend Ricardo suggests that "La fiesta brava" (Andrés's tale) reflects the influence of Carlos Fuentes's works, a major theme of which is the continuing vitality of the mythical past in present-day Mexican life. Andrés's preoccupation with the interpretations of his story and his guilty association with his protagonist draws him psychologically into its fictional framework, making his destiny and Keller's one and the same. Thus like most authors of self-conscious metafiction, Pacheco dramatizes the dialectic interplay between fiction and reality, blurring distinctions and imbuing each realm with elements of the other.

The *fiesta brava* is a term used to designate the sport of bullfighting, which the brutal Keller ironically rejects as a sign of savagery in the Mexican character. The story's title, however, points beyond this immediate connotation, emerging as a metaphor of the political and cultural conflicts between peoples throughout history. What distinguishes "La fiesta brava" from other *metaficciones* such as "El Aleph" and "Los babas del diablo" are its strong political overtones.

The dichotomy between reality and imagination becomes a major structural device in Gabriel García Márquez's tale, "El ahogado más hermoso del mundo" (1972; "The Handsomest Drowned Man in the World"), in which the gigantic corpse of a young man is washed ashore near a drab seaside village. While preparing his body for burial, the women of the village gaze at him in ecstasy, imagining him in real-life situations and even christening him Esteban. The elaborate funeral they prepare not only establishes a common bond among all the villagers but also convinces them that because of Esteban's brief appearance in their midst, their lives will undergo a dramatic change for the better.

The themes of purification and rebirth are clearly suggested by the dead man's gifts of beauty, hope, and solidarity to a community steeped in inertia. These themes are reinforced by poetic resonances of myth that enrich the story's literary fabric. Like a classic hero, Esteban arrives mysteriously, and like Odysseus, who also traversed the seas, he assumes superhuman proportions. The wailing women at Esteban's funeral and the sailor tied to the mast of a passing vessel recall Odysseus's efforts to resist the song of the Sirens when he was making his way back to Ithaca. Esteban also reveals certain similarities to Quetzalcoatl, who represented an enlightened form of religion and who would, according to legend, return to Mexico via the sea. Esteban's enormous size in comparison to the other men of the village reminds the reader of Gulliver's adventures among the Lilliputians.

The structural artistry of "El ahogado más hermoso del mundo" stems from the dialectical interplay between baroque, hyperbolic flights of imagination and simple, down-to-earth reality. The children play delightedly with the dead man's body, believing it to be a whale, until the more serious-minded adults discover it. The calm and bountiful sea that produced the marvelous stranger stands in sharp contrast to the arid, rocky village of only twenty houses; ecstatic over the sudden infusion of beauty into their lives, the women compare their husbands unfavorably with the godlike Esteban. After the latter is christened, however, he assumes more human proportions that alter their idealized perception of him and provoke sobs instead of sighs; the men react negatively to their wives' exaggerated grief, wanting to bury the body forthwith and forget it; and, in the final lines, the spiritual regeneration of the villagers, all of whom have become "kinsmen" through Esteban's inspiring presence, synthesizes the opposites enlivening the narrative thread. Also woven into the structure is the suggestion of cyclical time, as Esteban is returned to the sea wearing the trousers of an "undersized child"—implying a new beginning—and without an anchor in case he might choose to come back some day. Although allegedly written for children, this fictional eulogy to beauty, imagination, and human solidarity reveals esthetic qualities that expand its appeal to all age groups.

Since the military coup against Salvador Allende's socialist regime in September 1973, many Chilean writers have left their native land to continue their profession abroad.[6] Among the most promising of these is Antonio Skármeta (1940–   ), two of whose stories dramatize events in Chile before and after the coup. "Primera preparatoria" (1973; First Grade) is narrated in first person by a young intellectual whose older brother is leaving for Australia, apparently because of his objections to Allende's policies. The night before his departure he has had a violent quarrel with his Italian-born father who supports the liberal government and now refuses to bid farewell to his son. "La llamada" (1975; The Phone Call) portrays a timid professor of literature who at some time in the recent past was detained briefly by the military regime of General Augusto Pinochet. (Neither Pinochet nor Allende is mentioned by name in either story.) As he leaves the institute where he works, he is approached by two policemen, one of whom is his former student. After a short, unnerving conversation, he enters a cafe to make a telephone call, but on seeing a man sitting nearby reading a newspaper, he changes his mind and leaves.

Skármeta's technique, like that of Norberto Fuentes and Guillermo Cabrera Infante, is reminiscent of Hemingway's, consisting primarily of dialogue and simple narrative delivered by a direct, objective observer meant to stimulate the imagination and oblige the reader to discover possible cause and effect relationships from the limited material presented. In "Primera preparatoria" the father refers to the narrator's brother as a *reaccionario*, ("reactionary") but it is the latter's conservative dress, lack of interest in books (in contrast to the narrator), and decision to emigrate that suggest his opposition to Chile's left-wing government. His climactic, emotion-packed scene with his father and the narrator's cool farewell illustrate the impact on human relations of the tense political atmosphere providing the story's backdrop.

In "La llamada" the conversation of the three characters appears amiable on the surface, but an undercurrent of tension is revealed by the professor's jittery reactions to the false cordiality of the policemen. Dramatic tension mounts, with the ex-student's ironic reference to Pablo Neruda, who was a strong supporter of the Allende regime, and his parting remark that he and the sergeant will be dropping by the institute from time to time. In the final lines of the story the reader must decide if the man in the cafe is a spy or merely an innocent bystander in an atmosphere heavy with suspicion and fear. For Skármeta, it would seem, the suggestion of political oppression is more esthetically evocative than the description of acts of cruelty.

In 1947 Julio Cortázar published his first short story, "Casa tomada" ("House Taken Over"), in which a middle-aged bachelor shares a large home with his sister until their routine existence is abruptly ended by unnamed invaders who force them out into a world they are unprepared to face. "Verano" (1974; "Summer") is in some respects a reworking of the earlier tale, the protagonists being a childless couple, Mariano and Zulma, who, while vacationing in their cabin, agree to keep a friend's small daughter overnight. Late that evening a neighing horse gallops around the cabin, frightening the couple and arousing their erotic instincts. The next morning the appearance of normality is established once again.

"Verano" can be read as a psychological fantasy, the elements of Freudian and Jungian thought reinforcing those of the fantastic genre. The child's unexpected arrival at the country home of Mariano and Zulma disturbs the pattern of their existence, which is characterized by inflexible routine, lack of spontaneity, and alienation from each other. The little girl, who remains anonymous throughout the story, embodies imagination, her childlike innocence triggering Mariano's speculation that his and his wife's daily rituals are merely adult defense mechanisms against the chaos of death and nothingness. The horse probably symbolizes lust, but it could also represent the blind cosmic forces of chaos and, as Jung has stated, the magic, intuitive side of man, all of which in the present context suggests the rebellion of instinct and imagination against the banality of the protagonists' lives. This clash between the rational and irrational spheres creates an esthetically charged aura of ambiguity that endures at the end of the story, thus placing it unequivocally in the category of fantastic literature.

Mariano and Zulma typify Cortázar's protagonists, many of whose lives are disrupted by hallucinations, nightmares, and monstrous visions emanating from the hidden recesses of the selves they have sought to suppress through meaningless, repetitive activity. By dramatizing the precarious order of the rational world, Cortázar demonstrates his contempt for oppressive routine and its disastrous effects on the fragile personality. For his characters, fantasy often takes the form of self-liberation brought about by the revelation of the mysterious "other." Their liberation, however, is either momentary, as in the case of Mariano and Zulma, or destructive, as in "Casa tomada." Written in a direct, understated style, both tales convey the author's ironic vision of a world in which at any given moment fantasy can subvert objective, everyday life, either through a primitive, animistic mode of perception ("Verano") or the mysterious gothic invaders referred to only as "they" ("Casa tomada").

Just as Sorrentino is relatively unknown outside Argentina, the Mexican writer María Luisa Puga (1936–   ) has yet to reach an extensive audience beyond the borders of her native land. Her "Inmóvil sol secreto" (1979; Secret, Immobile Sun) depicts the strained relationship between the two lovers who flee to an island in Greece hoping to forget an incident from their past. Narrated in first person by the young woman whose infidelity is the cause of the tension between them, the story ends when Enrique finds himself unable to forgive her.

This extremely thin plot serves as the framework for a finely wrought dramatization of the precarious relationship. The island setting may be seen as a symbol of the characters' isolation from each other, whereas their past represents a smoldering threat that determines the plot's trajectory and culminates with a postcard from the narrator's former lover and her brief encounter with a gringo tourist. Puga captures the essence of the exotic setting by means of visual and olfactory imagery, but it is her poetically stylized insights into the protagonists' fluctuating states of mind that provide the story's literary underpinnings. On one occasion the narrator states that although a delicate and imperceptible bond is forming between them, she is unable to determine whether it is "companionship" or "solitude in very consoling company." Their daily swims, she believes, serve to bury their past by way of "a silent repetition" that also seems to inject life into their relationship. They return to the village holding hands, greeting the villagers and "building an image on which we try to lean." As the days pass, the narrator experiences a sensation of panic caused by "the frightful empty space" between each hour and "a vacuum" that little by little is consuming her existence. On her lover's face she detects the hurt expression she has learned to hate because it arouses her "pious compassion," which only drives them further apart.

The narrator's feelings of despair are given substance, and thus more poignancy, through metaphors combining abstract nouns and evocative verbs of action. "At times I am assaulted by a bitter laughter . . . because I see ourselves unwillingly dragging along this hope for a new life. And I find myself wanting to ventilate this present just as when I open the windows of the bedroom and shake the sheets aggressively. I want the sun to come in, the wind to wash these secret reticences that are born each night."

The narrator also realizes that when Enrique makes love to her he is seeking "the disintegration of another presence," her infidelity, and that he is not seeking her but rather a renewed image of himself. Thus when the postcard from her former lover terminates the present affair, her "other presence" assumes possession of her wounded ego and, immersed in a kind of dreamlike vertigo, she joins her gringo admirer. "Inmóvil sol secreto" is a skillfully executed portrait of jealousy and its nefarious effects by one of the bright new talents on today's Spanish American literary horizon.

A story that seems particularly representative of the early 1980s is one written by Carlos Fuentes (1929–   ), Mexico's best living writer of fiction and one of Latin America's most significant men of letters. The undying influence of the Mexican past, both pre-Hispanic and colonial, on present-day reality is a theme Fuentes has developed in several of his works by means of simultaneous, intersecting temporal planes. In "Chac Mool" (1954; "Chac-Mool"), his most popular tale, an idol representing the Mayan and Toltec rain god comes to life and claims the protagonist as a sacrificial victim.

The colonial period is evoked in "Estos fueron los palacios" (1980; "These Were Palaces"), which portrays a lonely retired servant, Manuela, and her friend, a crippled fourteen-year-old youth named Luisito, both of whom live in a tenement near the Zocalo in Mexico City. A sensitive realist, Manuela feeds the stray dogs in the neighborhood and treats them when they are hurt, whereas the more romantically inclined Luisito spends his days envisioning the majestic past of his once-wealthy family and that of colonial Mexico when the tenements around the Zocalo were beautiful palaces. A mysterious, intuitive understanding develops between the two lonely protagonists, who need and complement each other in a variety of ways. Luisito not only replaces, in Manuela's mind, the daughter she has lost, but also induces her to imagine the grandeur of past centuries instead of reliving her own difficult life as a servant in the household of a general. Manuela's spiritual strength, moreover, compensates for Luisito's physical infirmity, making him more aware of life around him and thus allowing him to achieve a greater sense of identity. The tenement and the dogs symbolize legacies of the past, the former having derived from an affluent social class condemned to decay, and the latter representing the base of Mexico's societal pyramid built up through generations of cruelty, injustice, and poverty.

The final episodes of the story are especially revealing. In the dream-like atmosphere of a moonlit night Manuela and Luisito descend the main staircase of their "palace" to the sounds of the barking dogs—a symbol of the present—and of beautiful music out of the remote past. Their subsequent dance reinforces the link between time levels when Manuela evokes her former lover and tells Luisito to imagine that he is embracing her beautiful daughter Lupe Lupita, who disappeared many years previously. The fading of the music and the increasingly strident barking of the dogs, whom Manuela and Luisito vow they will always care for, propel the action completely into the present and suggest a social message. The final scene in which Luisito goes alone to the kitchen for food despite his handicap indicates that he has taken a significant step in the maturation process. Unlike "Chac Mool," whose protagonist becomes a victim of the indigenous past, "Estos fueron los palacios" challenges Mexicans to overcome the crippling legacy of the conquest embodied in Luisito and master their own destiny.

Conclusions

Looking back over the past four decades of Spanish American short fiction, one is impressed by the wide variety of themes and techniques as well as by the generally high quality of the genre. From the metaphysical tales of Borges, who expunged the dead wood encumbering

Spanish American prose, many writers have learned greater respect for linguistic precision and, perhaps somewhat paradoxically, a fundamental skepticism toward language as a tool for mirroring reality. Thus many fine practitioners have rejected traditional realism for surrealism, fantasy, metafiction, the Absurd, or the grotesque to express their esthetic ideals and philosophical preoccupations. The psychological tale has attained new heights of excellence, with greater stress given to existential solitude, Jungian archetypes, and portraits of the alter ego or double. Also significant is a group of stories dealing with the political and social conflicts so common throughout much of Spanish American history, themes often conveyed in a direct, realistic style. Even in these stories, however, humor, irony, and elliptical ambiguity have tended to replace the tedious verbosity of much traditional social protest literature.

The most effective stylistic and structural devices used to capture the complex realities of today's world include the shifting point of view, the interior monologue, and the art of juxtaposition or montage, all of which also stretch, fragment, circularize, or destroy lineal time. The authors of modern short fiction often reject sequential action, preferring to present their materials in the form of incomplete mosaics that oblige the reader to link seemingly unrelated segments to discover intended meanings. Thus just as the protagonist of "Las babas del diablo" recreates his story while gazing at an enlarged snapshot, the reader must project his imagination beyond the immediate limitations of the fictional framework to supply the missing segments of the mosaic. Structural unity, then, remains intact but concealed by subtly manipulated techniques.

Although Borges is still the undisputed master of the genre, Cortázar has emerged as an exceptionally gifted weaver of fantasies whose prestige is beginning to approach that of his elder compatriot. The reputations of other established men of letters such as Carpentier, Onetti, Arreola, Rulfo, Donoso, García Márquez, and Fuentes have spread well beyond the Spanish-speaking world. Many younger writers whose works have yet to be translated will undoubtedly soon reach wider audiences both within and outside their native lands.

Many names worthy of notice have unfortunately been omitted. Among these are Antonio de Benedetto (1922–   ), Humberto Constantini (1924–   ), and Luisa Valenzuela (1938–   ), of Argentina; Renato Prada Oropesa (1937–   ), of Bolivia; Enrique Lafourcade (1927–   ) and Jorge Edwards (1931–   ) of Chile; Manuel Mejía Vallejo (1923–   ) and Oscar Collazos (1942–   ) of Colombia;

Yolanda Oreamuno (1917–   ) and Fabián Dobles (1918–   ) of
Costa Rica; Humberto Arenal (1926–   ) of Cuba; César Dávila
Andrade (1937–   ) of Ecuador; Rosario Castellanos (1925–1974)
and Jorge Ibargüengoitia (1928–   ) of Mexico; Sergio Ramírez
(1942–   ) of Nicaragua; Oswaldo Reynoso (1932–   ) and Mario
Vargas Llosa (1936–   ) of Peru; Mario Benedetti (1920–   ) of
Uruguay; and Salvador Garmendia (1928–   ) and Adriano Gonzá-
lez León (1931–   ) of Venezuela.

The contemporary Spanish American short story has demonstrated a
remarkable degree of sophistication and originality primarily because
of the universality of its Weltanschauung and the experimental, avant-
garde nature of its form. The seminal works of the 1940s and 1950s were
followed by an explosion of talent during the 1960s, a period of economic prosperity and political ferment. Although the 1970s have seen a
slackening of this so-called boom, familiar figures are continuing to
write short stories and newcomers are offering fresh insights into human
behavior as well as new levels of contact with reality. This combination
of time-tested creativity and esthetic discovery augurs well for the
future of the genre.

George R. McMurray
Colorado State University, Fort Collins

Notes and References

MAJOR FIGURES IN THE BRAZILIAN SHORT STORY

1. In the text the date in parentheses that follows titles of stories and of collections refers to book, not journal, publication. If the collection has been translated into English, the title apears in italics; if the story has been translated, its title appears in quotation marks.

2. David William Foster, "Joaquin Maria Machado de Assis," in *Critical Survey of Short Fiction* (Englewood Cliffs, N.J.: Salem Press, 1981), pp. 1849–53. Metafiction, as a subcategory of metaliterature, refers to a work that articulates, either obliquely or explicitly, a preoccupation with the nature of fiction, particularly the difficulties of capturing experience through literary art and the ways in which literary art becomes a distortion rather than an accurate representation of experience.

3. David William Foster, "João Guimaraês Rosa," in *Critical Survey of Short Fiction*, 1563–68.

4. I should like to acknowledge the suggestions for this chapter made so generously by Naomi Lindstrom of the University of Texas at Austin and Roberto Reis of the Universadade de Gama Filho in Rio de Janeiro.

THE SPANISH AMERICAN SHORT STORY FROM ECHEVERRÍA TO QUIROGA

1. Enrique Anderson Imbert makes this comment in his *Spanish American Literature, A History,* trans. John V. Falconieri (Detroit, 1963), p. 211.

2. Noe Jitrik's objections to Payró's language of narration are expressed in "Socialismo y gracia en Roberto J. Payró" [Socialism and wit in Roberto J. Payró], in his *El fuego de la especie* [Fire of the species] (Buenos Aires: Siglo XXI, 1971), pp. 99–127; see especially 110–14.

3. Octavio Paz's explanation of the metaphysical and theosophical underpinnings of modernist thought, and of how these notions corresponded to the work of producing a more rhythmic literary language, appear in *Cuadrivio* (Quadrivium) (Mexico City: Joaquín Mortiz, 1965), especially "El caracol y la sirena" [The siren and the seashell], pp. 11–65, and "El camino de la pasión" [The route of passion], pp. 69–130. In English, see *The Siren and the Seashell*

and Other Essays, trans. Lysander Kemp and Margaret Sayers Peden (Austin: University of Texas Press, 1973) for Paz's orienting remarks concerning the modernist phenomenon. For a briefer commentary containing Paz's main ideas on modernism, see his "Prologue" to Lysander Kemp translation, *Selected Poems of Rubén Darío* (Austin: University of Texas Press, 1979), pp. 7–18.

4. Jorge Luis Borges, *Leopoldo Lugones* (Buenos Aires: Pleamar, 1965), p. 12.

THE SPANISH AMERICAN SHORT STORY FROM QUIROGA TO BORGES

1. Horacio Quiroga, *Cuentos,* ed. R. Lazo (Mexico City: Porrúa, 1968, p. xxxiv. The decalogue appears in English in William Peden's "Some Notes on Quiroga's Stories," *Review* (Winter 1976): 41–43.

2. The dates of the Quiroga stories refer to the year of journal publication to emphasize the chronologic span of his work and the dates of different kinds of stories.

3. See Luis Leal, *Historia del cuento hispanoamericano,* (Mexico City, 1966) p. 69.

4. Ibid., p. 105.

5. Seymour Menton, *El cuento hispanoamericano,* (Mexico City, 1970), 2:112–14.

6. Leal, p. 97.

7. Menton, 1:312–14.

THE SPANISH AMERICAN SHORT STORY FROM BORGES TO THE PRESENT

1. See D.P. Gallagher's chapter on Borges in his *Modern Latin American Literature* (New York: Oxford University Press, 1973), pp. 94–121.

2. Zeno of Elea's "Dichotomy" is referred to here. According to his paradox, before a body in motion can reach a given point it must first traverse half of the distance; before it can traverse half it must traverse a quarter; and so on ad infinitum. Hence for a body to pass from one point to another it must traverse an infinite number of divisions. Theoretically, then, a goal can never be reached. When Lönnrot tells Scharlach to look for him at a certain point on a straight line, he is implying that in the infinite maze of eternity Scharlach will never be able to find him.

3. Todorov defines the fantastic as a state of uncertainty experienced by the reader because of the text's violation of natural laws. If the violation can be explained by the influence of an illusion, the laws of reality remain intact, and the text represents an example of the uncanny (*l'étrange*). If the violation of natural laws is due to the imposition of supernatural laws beyond the reader's experience (which is the case in "Paulina"), the text becomes an example of the marvelous. The fantastic, then, occupies the narrow, and often tenuous, realm of ambiguity between the uncanny and the marvelous. See Todorov's *The*

Fantastic: A Structuralist Approach to a Literary Genre (Ithaca, N.Y.: Cornell University Press, 1975), pp. 24–40.

Barrenechea sees the fantastic in broader terms, defining it as the confrontation between abnormal events and everyday reality. Consult her "Ensayo de una tipología de la literatura fantástica," *Revista Iberoamericana* 80 (July–September 1972): 391–403.

4. For a variety of critical views on magical realism, see *Otros mundos otros fuegos*, ed. Donald A. Yates (East Lansing, Mich.: Latin American Studies Center, 1975). Also the Spring-Summer 1981 issue of *Colorado State Review* 8:2 devoted to the subject of magical realism.

5. I am grateful to Professor Thomas C. Meehan for allowing me to read the chapter on Sorrentino from the manuscript of his forthcoming book, *Essays on Argentine Narrators* (Valencia: Albatros Ediciones, 1982).

6. For a sampling of fiction by Chileans in exile, see the anthology, *Joven narrativa chilena después del golpe*, ed. Antonio Skármeta (Clear Creek, Ind.: American Hispanist, 1976). In addition to Skármeta, prominent writers of this group include Poli Délano (1936–   ), Luis Domínguez (1933–   ), and Hernán Valdés (1934–   ).

Bibliography

Selected Listing of Anthologies and Individual Collections of Latin American Short Stories in English
Anthologies are denoted by an asterisk*.

Arreola, Juan José. *Confabulario and Other Inventions*. Translated by George D. Schade. Austin: University of Texas Press, 1964.

*Babín, María Teresa, and Steiner, Stan, eds. *Borinquen: An Anthology of Puerto Rican Literature*. New York: Alfred A. Knopf, 1974.

Bioy Casares, Adolfo. *The Invention of Morel; and other stories* from La trama celeste. Translated by Ruth L. C. Simms. Austin: University of Texas Press, 1964.

Bombal, María Luisa. *New Islands*. Translated by Richard Cunningham. New York: Farrar, Straus & Giroux, 1982.

Borges, Jorge Luis. *The Aleph and Other Stories: 1933–1969*. Edited and translated by Norman Thomas de Giovanni (in collaboration with the author). New York: E. P. Dutton, 1970.

————. *Doctor Brodie's Report*. Translated by Norman Thomas di Giovanni. New York: E.P. Dutton, 1972.

————. *Ficciones*. Edited by Anthony Kerrigan. New York: Grove Press, 1962.

————. *Labyrinths; Selected Stories and Other Writings*. Edited by Donald A. Yates and James E. Irby. New York: New Directions, 1964.

Carpentier, Alejo. *War of Time*. Translated by Frances Partridge. New York: Alfred A. Knopf, 1970.

*Carpentier, Hortense, and Brof, Janet, eds. *Doors and Mirrors; Fiction and Poetry from Spanish America, 1920–1970*. New York: Grossman Press, 1972.

*Carranza, Sylvia, and Cazabon, María Juana, eds. *Cuban Short Stories 1959–1966*. Havana: Book Institute, 1967.

*Cohen, J. M., ed. *Latin American Writing of Today*. Harmondsworth: Penguin Books, 1967.

*Colford, William Ed., ed., and trans. *Classic Tales from Spanish America*. New York: Barron's Educational Service, 1962.

————. *A Change of Light and Other Stories*. Translated by Gregory Rabassa. New York: Alfred A. Knopf, 1980.

Cortázar, Julio. All Fires the Fire, and Other Stories. Translated by Suzanne Jill Levine. New York: Pantheon Books, 1973.
————. End of the Game, and Other Stories. Translated by Paul Blackburn. New York: Pantheon Books, 1967.
*deOnis, Harriet. The Golden Land: An Anthology of Latin American Folklore in Literature. New York: Alfred A. Knopf, 1948.
Donoso, José. Charleston: & Other Stories. Translated by Andrée Conrad. Boston: David R. Godine, 1977.
*Donoso, José, and Henkin, William, eds. The TriQuarterly Anthology of Contemporary Latin American Literature. New York: E. P. Dutton, 1969. Originally a special isue of TriQuarterly (Fall-Winter 1968–69).
*Flakoll, Darwin J., and Alegría, Claribel, eds. New Voices of Hispanic America: An Anthology. Boston: Beacon Press, 1962.
*Flores, Angel, and Poore, Dudley, eds. Fiesta in November. Boston: Houghton Mifflin Company, 1942.
*Franco, Jean, ed. Short Stories in Spanish. Cuentos Hispánicos. Harmondsworth: Penguin Books, 1966.
*Frank, Waldo. Tales from the Argentine. Translated by Anita Brenner. New York: Farrar and Rinehart, 1930.
*Fremantle, Anne, ed. Latin America Literature Today. New York: New American Library, 1977.
Fuentes, Carlos. Burnt Water. Translated by Margaret Sayers Peden. New York: Farrar, Straus & Giroux, 1980.
Fuentes, Carlos; Donoso, José; and Sarduy, Severo. Triple Cross. Translated by Suzanne Jill Levine and Hallie D. Taylor. New York: E. P. Dutton & Co., 1972.
García Márquez, Gabriel. The Innocent Eréndira, and Other Stories. Translated by Gregory Rabassa. New York: Harper & Row, 1978.
————. Leaf Storm, and Other Stories. Translated by Gregory Rabassa. New York: Harper & Row, 1972.
————. No One Writes to the Colonel, and Other Stories. Translated by J. S. Bernstein. New York: Harper & Row, 1968.
*Goldberg, Isaac, ed. and trans. Brazilian Tales. New York: Alfred A. Knopf, 1922.
*Grossman, William L., ed. and trans. Modern Brazilian Short Stories. Berkeley: University of California Press, 1968.
*Howes, Barbara, ed. The Eye of the Heart. New York: Bobbs Merrill, 1973.
*Jones, Willis Knapp, ed. Spanish-American Literature in Translation, a selection of Poetry, Fiction and Drama since 1888. New York: Ungar, 1963.
*Lawaetz, Gudie, ed. Short Stories 2/Cuentos Hispánicos 2. Harmondsworth: Penguin Books, 1972.
Lillo, Baldomero. The Devil's Pit, and Other Stories by Baldomero Lillo. Translated by Esther S. Dillon. Washington, D.C.: Organization of American States, 1959.

Lima Barreto, Alfonso Henrique de. *Lima Barreto, Bibliography and Transla-tions.* Edited by Maria Luisa Nunes. Boston: G. K. Hall, 1979.
Lispector, Clarice. *Family Ties.* Translated by Giovanni Pontiero. Austin: Uni-versity of Texas Press, 1972.
Lobato, José Bento Monteiro. *Brazilian Short Stories (Stories from Urupês).* Girard, Kans.: Haldeman-Julius, 1925.
Machado de Assis, Joaquin Maria de. *The Devil's Church and Other Stories.* Translated by Jack Schmitt and Lorie Ishimatsu. Austin: University of Texas Press, 1977.
———. *The Psychiatrist, and Other Stories.* Translated by William L. Grossman and Helen Caldwell. Berkeley: University of California Press, 1963.
*Mancini, Pat McNees, ed. *Contemporary Latin American Short Stories.* Greenwich, Conn.: Fawcett, 1974.
*Menton, Seymour, ed. *The Spanish American Short Story: A Critical Anthol-ogy.* Berkeley: University of California Press, 1980.
Palma, Ricardo. *The Knights of the Cape and Thirty-Seven Other Selections from the Tradiciones Peruanas of Ricardo Palma.* Translated by Harriet de Onís. New York: Alfred A. Knopf, 1945.
Prize Stories from Latin America, by the Winners of the Life en español Contest. Garden City, N.Y.: Doubleday, 1963.
Quiroga, Horacio. *The Decapitated Chicken and Other Stories.* Edited and translated by Margaret Sayers Peden. Austin: University of Texas Press, 1976.
*Rodriguez Monegal, Emir, ed. with the assistance of Thomas Colchie. *The Borzoi Anthology of Latin American Literature.* New York: Alfred A. Knopf, 1977.
Rosa, João Guimarães. *The Third Bank of the River, and Other Stories.* Translated by Barbara Shelby. New York: Alfred A. Knopf, 1968.
Rulfo, Juan. *The Burning Plain, and Other Stories.* Translated by George D. Schade. Austin: University of Texas Press, 1967.
*Schulte, Rainer, ed. *Mundus Artium* (Summer 1970).
Soto, Pedro Juan. *Spiks.* Translated by Victoria Ortiz. New York: Monthly Review Press, 1973.
*Torres-Ríoseco, Arturo, ed. *Short Stories of Latin America.* New York: Las Americas Publishing Co., 1963.
Trevisan, Dalton. *The Vampire of Curitiba and Other Stories.* Translated by Gregory Rabassa. New York: Alfred A. Knopf, 1972.
*Troupe, Quincy, and Schulte, Rainer, eds. *Giant Talk: An Anthology of Third World Writings.* New York: Vintage Books, 1975.
Valenzuela, Luisa. *Clara: Thirteen Short Stories and a Novel.* Translated by Hortense Carpentier. New York: Harcourt Brace Jovanovich, 1979.
———. *Strange Things Happen Here: Twenty-six Short Stories and a Novel.* Translated by Helen Lane. New York: Harcourt Brace Jovanovich, 1979.

Vargas Llosa, Mario. *The Cubs and Other Stories*. Translated by Gregory Kolovakos and Ronald Christ. New York: Harper & Row, 1979.

Veiga, José J. *The Misplaced Machine and Other Stories*. Translated by Pamela Bird. New York: Alfred A. Knopf, 1970.

*Wagenheim, Kal, ed. *Cuentos: An Anthology of Short Stories from Puerto Rico*. New York: Schocken Books, 1978.

Yates, Donald A., ed. *Latin Blood: The Best Crime and Detective Stories of South America*. New York: Nerder & Nerder, 1972.

Selected Source Books and Book-Length Critical Studies in English

Alazraki, Jaime. *Jorge Luis Borges*. New York: Columbia University Press, 1971. A brief, but exceptionally good, introduction to Borges's fiction.

Alaziaki, Jaime, and Ivask, Ivor, eds. *The Final Island*. Norman: University of Oklahoma Press, 1978. Series of essays by Cortázar scholars and friends; proceedings of International Symposium held at the University of Oklahoma in 1976.

Aldrich, Earl M., Jr. *The Modern Short Story in Peru*. Madison: University of Wisconsin Press, 1966. Good comments on the Peruvian generation of the 1950s.

Anderson Imbert, Enrique. *Spanish American Literature: A History*. Translated by John V. Falconieri. Detroit: Wayne State University, 1963. General overview; basic source in regard to names and dates.

Barrenechea, Ana María. *Borges the Labyrinth Maker*. Edited and translated by Robert Lima. New York: New York University Press, 1965. A seminal thematic study of Borges's fiction.

Brody, Robert, and Rossman, Charles, eds. *Carlos Fuentes: A Collection of Critical Essays*. Austin: University of Texas Press, 1982. Essays on all aspects of Fuentes's writing, including collections of short stories.

Caldwell, Helen. *Machado de Assis: The Brazilian Master and His Novels*. Berkeley: University of California Press, 1970. The standard study in English on Machado in terms of biography as well as themes.

Christ, Ronald J. *The Narrow Act: Borges' Art of Allusion*. New York: New York University Press, 1969. Concentrates on allusion as the key to understanding Borges; basically a comparative approach.

Cohen, J.M. *Jorge Luis Borges*. Edinburgh: Oliver & Boyd, 1973. Basic introduction by a well-known translator and writer. Historical background and critical analyses.

Dunham, Lowell, and Ivask, Ivor, eds. *The Cardinal Points of Borges*. Norman: University of Oklahoma Press, 1971. Series of essays by Borges scholars and friends; proceedings of International Symposium held at the University of Oklahoma in 1969.

Foster, David William. *Augusto Roa Bastos*. Boston: Twayne Publishers, 1978. A general study of Roa Bastos's work, including several of his stories.

————. *A Dictionary of Contemporary Latin American Authors*. Tempe: Center for Latin American Studies, Arizona State University, 1975. Basic source book for general information.

————. *Studies in the Contemporary Spanish American Short Story*. Columbia: University of Missouri Press, 1979. Close reading of selected stories, largely structuralist and semiotic study.

Foster, David William, and Foster, Virginia Ramos. *Modern Latin American Literature*. New York: Frederic Ungar, 1975. 2 vols. A selection of representative criticism on major modern authors.

Foster, David William, and Reis, Roberto. *A Dictionary of Contemporary Brazilian Authors*. Tempe: Center for Latin American Studies, Arizona State University, 1982. Dictionary format, critical analyses of over one hundred contemporary Brazilian writers.

Franco, Jean. *An Introduction to Spanish American Literature*. Cambridge: Cambridge University Press, 1969. History of the literature by a major British critic.

Freudenthal, Juan R., and Freudenthal, Patricia M., eds. *Index to Anthologies of Latin American Literature in English Translation*. Boston: G. K. Hall, 1977. Provides access to one hundred and sixteen anthologies.

Gallagher, D. P. *Modern Latin American Literature*. London: Oxford University Press, 1973. Contains excellent discussions of Borges's, García Márquez's, and Cabrera Infante's works.

Garfield, Evelyn Picon. *Julio Cortázar*. New York: Frederick Ungar, 1975. General study of Cortázar's fiction, including some of his best-known stories.

Garganigo, John F. *Javier de Viana*. Boston: Twayne Publishers, 1972. Introduction to de Viana's works; study of his stories.

Goldberg, Isaac. *Brazilian Literature*. New York: Alfred A. Knopf, 1922. Chapter 2 of Part 2 is an early introduction in English to the importance of Machado de Assis.

González Echevarría, Roberto. *Alejo Carpentier: The Pilgrim at Home*. Ithaca: Cornell University Press, 1977. Examines this major author in the context of a "primarily post-Romantic literary tradition."

Gonazález-Gerth, Miguel, and Schade, George. *Rubén Darío, Centennial Studies*. Austin: Institute for Latin American Studies, University of Texas, 1970. Five lectures given during the 1967 centenary celebration, with common themes of the ancient identification of poet and prophet.

Kadir, Djelal. *Juan Carlos Onetti*. Boston: Twayne Publishers, 1977. A general study of Onetti's works, including some of his stories.

Martín, Eleanor J. *Rene Marqués*. Boston: Twayne Publishers, 1979. General study of Marqués's work, including his stories.

McMurray, George R. *Gabriel García Márquez.* New York: Frederick Ungar, 1977. General study of García Márquez's work, including all his stories.

———. *Jorge Luis Borges.* New York: Frederick Ungar, 1980. An introductory discussion of the principal themes and techniques in Borges's fiction.

———. *José Donoso.* Boston: Twayne Publishers, 1979. General study of Donoso's work, including all of his stories.

Menton, Seymour. *Prose Fiction of the Cuban Revolution.* Austin: University of Texas Press, 1975. Contains a section on the recent Cuban short story, with emphasis on the generation of 1970.

Murillo, L. A. *The Cyclical Night: Irony in James Joyce and Jorge Luis Borges.* Cambridge: Harvard University Press, 1968. Two separate essays. Murillo suggests that technical and philosophical traits link these two giants, but many dissimilarities discourage a strictly comparative study.

Peden, Margaret Sayers. "Translation." In *Handbook of Latin American Studies,* ed. Dolores M. Martin, vol. 40. Gainesville: University Presses of Florida, 1978. Bibliography.

———. "Translation." In *Handbook of Latin American Studies,* ed. Dolores M. Martin, vol. 42. Austin: University of Texas Press, 1980. Bibliography.

Polt, John. *The Writings of Eduardo Mallea.* Berkeley: University of California Press, 1959. Basic study of Mallea's art and ideas.

Shaw, Bradley, A. *Latin American Literature in English Translation: An Annotated Bibiliography.* New York: New York University Press, 1976. Basic resource book for translations into English.

———. *Latin American Literature in English 1975–1978.* New York: Center for Inter-American Relations, 1979. Update of earlier publication.

Souza, Raymond D. *Lino Novás Calvo.* Boston: Twayne Publishers, 1981. Basic introductory study of all aspects of Novás Calvo's work.

Stabb, Martin S. *Jorge Luis Borges.* Boston: Twayne Publishers, 1970. Introduction to Borges the man, poet, and essayist, as well as author of prose fiction; includes critical reactions.

Studies in Short Fiction 8, no. 1 (1971). Contains twenty-four essays of good quality on the modern Latin American short story.

Sturrock, John. *Paper Tigers. The Ideal Fictions of Jorge Luis Borges.* Oxford: Oxford University Press, 1977. Believes Borges is at his best in his fictions, which he finds most original in having arisen from intractable and arid problems in metaphysics.

Vincent, John. *João Guimarães Rosa.* Boston: Twayne Publishers, 1978. An authoritative study followed by an annotated bibliography of major criticism.

Wheelock, Carter. *The Mythmaker: A Study of Motif and Symbol in the Short Stories of Jorge Luis Borges.* Austin: University of Texas Press, 1969. Study based on myth as "thought form"; argues that Borges's esthetic is one of the intelligence in which dreaming is equivalent to thinking.

Selected Critical Articles in English

Alazraki, Jaime. "Kabbalistic Traits in Borges' Narration." *Studies in Short Fiction* 8, no. 1 (1971):78–92. Excellent discussion of how Kabbalistic features contribute to enriching the ambiguity of Borges's fictions.

Aldrich, Earl M., Jr. "Recent Trends in the Peruvian Short Story." *Studies in Short Fiction* 8, no. 1 (1971):20–31. Good introduction to the Peruvian short story since 1950.

Alvarez Gardeazábal, Gustavo. "The Short Story in Colombia." *Review* 24 (1979):70–80. Brief introduction followed by stories of Marco Tulio, Aguilera Garramuño, Leopoldo Berdella de la Espriella, Juan Alberto Gutiérrez Moros, and David Sánchez Juliao.

Borgeson, Paul W., Jr. "The Turbulent Flow: Stream of Consciousness Techniques in the Short Stories of Juan Rulfo." *Revista de Estudios Hispánicos* 13, no. 2 (1979):226–52. Very good discussion of stylistic techniques in Rulfo's stories.

Callan, Richard J. "Animals as Mana Figures in José Donoso's 'Paseo' and 'Santelices.'" *Essays in Literature* 2, no. 1 (1975):115–22. Excellent study of Jungian elements in two of Donoso's best stories.

————. "Miguel Angel Asturias: Spokesman of His People." *Studies in Short Fiction* 8, no. 1 (1971):92–102. Describes how Austurias represents the Indian culture of Guatemala through myths, legends, and supernatural events.

Cortázar, Julio. "Poe as Poet and Story-writer." *Review* 17 (1976):42–46. Cortázar reveals a great many of his own precepts about the form in this study of the North American master.

Davis, Mary E. "The Voyage Beyond the Map: 'El ahogado más hermoso del mundo.'" *Kentucky Romance Quarterly* 26, no. 2 (1979):25–33. Very perceptive comments on mythical and literary allusions in García Márquez's story.

Deredita, John F. "The Shorter Works of Juan Carlos Onetti." *Studies in Short Fiction* 8, no. 1 (1971):112–22. Valuable introduction into lesser known aspect of Onetti's writing.

Earle, Peter G. "Dreams of Creation: Short Fiction in Spanish America." *University of Denver Quarterly* 12 (1977):67–79. Discusses the trajectory from realism to dreamlike reality in Borges, Rulfo, Cortázar, Donoso, Fuentes, and García Márquez.

"Focus on Horacio Quiroga." *Review* 19 (1976):27–46. Chronology; articles by Ernesto Montenegro, George Garrett, William Peden; translation of Quiroga's "The Flies."

"Focus on Jorge Luis Borges." *Review* 8 (1973):6–36. Chronology and guide by Norman Thomas de Giovanni; articles by Amado Alonso, David Gallagher, Suzanne Jill Levine, Roger Caillois, and Emir Rodriguez Monegal.

"Focus on Julio Cortázar." *Review* 7 (1972):14–35. Articles by J. M. Alonso, Evelyn Picon Garfield, Emir Rodriguez Monegal, C.D.B. Bryan, and Alfred J. MacAdam; "Snapshots of *Blow-up.*"

Foster, David William. "João Guimarães Rosa." In *Critical Survery of Short Fiction* (Englewood Cliffs, N.J.: Salem Press, 1981), pp. 1563–68. An introduction to Rosa's fiction and analysis of the story "As margens da alegria."

—————. "Joaquim Maria Machado de Assis." In *Critical Survey of Short Fiction* (Englewood Cliffs, N.J.: Salem Press, 1981), pp. 1849–1953. An introduction to Machado's fiction and an analysis of the story "*Singular ocorrência.*"

Gallagher, D. P. "The Novels and Short Stories of Adolfo Bioy Casares." *Bulletin of Hispanic Studies* 52, no. 3 (1975):247–66. Stresses the elements of comedy, parody, and irony in Bioy Casares's work.

Gilgen, Read G. "Absurdist Techniques in the Short Stories of Juan José Arreola." *Journal of Spanish Studies: Twentieth Century* 8, no. 1–2 (1980):67–77. Concentrates on Arreola's distorted and fantastic views of reality to convey absurdity.

————— "The Short Story of the Absurd: Spanish America's Contribution to Absurdist Literature." *Romance Notes* 18 (1977):164–68. Comments on the philosophy of the Absurd and its application to several Spanish American writers.

Gyruko, Lanin A. "Cyclic Time and Blood Sacrifice in Three Stories by Cortázar." *Revista Hispánica Moderna* 35 (1979):341–62. Perceptive comments on "La noche boca arriba," "Todos los fuegos el fuego," and "El ídolo de las Cícladas."

Johnston, Craig P. "Irony and the Double in Short Fiction by Julio Cortázar and Severo Sarduy." *Journal of Spanish Studies: Twentieth Century* 5, no. 2 (1977):111–22. Study of individual and his double, using irony to intensify the author's vision of man and his crisis of consciousness.

Langford, Walter M. "The Short Story in Mexico." *Kentucky Foreign Language Quarterly* 1, no. 1 (1954):52–59. Early study focusing on latter half of nineteenth century and first years of twentieth, particularly Rafael Muñoz and Agustín Yáñez.

Leal, Luis. "The New Mexican Short Story." *Studies in Short Fiction* 8, no. 1 (1971):9–19. Presents Juan José Arreola and Juan Rulfo as precursors of contemporary Mexican short fiction.

Massaud, Moisés. "Clarice Lispector: Fiction and Cosmic Vision." *Studies in Short Fiction* 8, no. 1 (1971):268–81. Explores the alienation and existentialism traditionally linked to Lispector's writing.

McMurray, George R. "Albert Camus's Concept of the Absurd and Juan José Arreola's 'The Switchman.'" *Latin American Literary Review* 7, no. 11

(1977):30–35. Specific examination of effects of Camus's philosophy on Arreola; close reading of Arreola's story.

Menton, Seymour. "Juan José Arreola and the Twentieth Century Short Story." *Hispania* 42, no. 3 (1959):295–308. Studies *Confabulario* and *Varia invención*; describes how Arreola moves from depths of existential despair to skepticism of magical realism.

———. "The Short Story of the Cuban Revolution, 1959–1969." *Studies in Short Fiction* 8, no. 1 (1971):32–43. History of Cuban short story and focus on post-Revolution *cuentistas*.

Paz, Octavio. "Prologue." In *Selected Poems of Rubén Darío*. Translated by Lysander Kemp. Austin: University of Texas Press, 1965, pp. 7–18. Recommended to readers confused by the apparent frivolity of modernist writing.

Peavler, Terry J. "Guillermo Cabrera Infante's Debt to Ernest Hemingway." *Hispania* 62 (1979):289–96. Compares Cabrera Infante's and Hemingway's literary styles.

Peden, Margaret Sayers. "The Arduous Journey." In *Symposium on the Short Story*. Lubbock: Texas Tech University Press, 1982. Approaches criticism of short story through vehicle of translation.

Peel, Roger M. "The Short Stories of Gabriel García Márquez." *Studies in Short Fiction* 8, no. 1 (1971):159–68. Further examination of the Macondo of *Cien años de soledad* in García Márquez's brief prose.

Pupo-Walker, Enrique. "The Contemporary Short Fiction of Spanish America: An Introductory Note." *Studies in Short Fiction* 8, no. 1 (1971):1–8. General overview of the form, and emphasis on affinity of Spanish American authors for short fiction.

Reedy, Daniel R. "the Symbolic Reality of Cortázar's 'Las babas del diablo.'" *Revista Hispánica Moderna* 36, no. 4 (1970–71):224–37. Excellent study of mythical elements in Cortázar's tales.

Reeve, Richard M. "Carlos Fuentes and the New Short Story in Mexico." *Studies in Short Fiction* 8, no. 1 (1971):169–79. Study of *Los días enmascarados, Cantar de ciegos, Aura,* and a few uncollected stories.

Rodríguez-Peralta, Phyllis. "Liberal Undercurrents in Palma's *Tradiciones peruanas*." *Revista de Estudios Hispánicos* 15, no. 2 (1981):283–97. Places Palma's sympathies with rebellious *criollo* against vain Spanish *hidalgo*. Argues the *Tradiciones* set the stage for appreciation of complex mixture of Peruvian society.

Rosenfeld, Anatole. "The Creative Narrative Processes of Osman Lins." *Studies in Short Fiction* 8, no. 1 (1971):230–44. Excellent introduction to the experimental stories of the 1950s and 1960s.

Severino, Alexandrino E. "Major Trends in the Development of the Brazilian Short Story." *Studies in Short Fiction* 8, no. 1 (1971):199–208. Survey of the form from its beginnings with Machado de Assis up to Trevisan, Fonseca, Lispector, Lins, and Guimarães Rosa.

Skármeta, Antonio. "Words Are My Home: Prose and Poetry by Young Chileans of the Late Seventies." *Review* 27 (1980):8–10. Discusses major writers inside and outside Chile since the military coup in 1973.

Wheelock, Carter. "Fantastic Symbolism in the Spanish American Short Story." *Hispanic Review* 48, no. 4 (1980):415–34. A systematic discussion of fantasy in the Spanish American short story from the 1850s into the 1960s, concluding with several of Cortázar's best-known tales.

Williams, Shirley A. "Prisoners of the Past: Three Fuentes Short Stories from *Los días enmascarados.*" *Journal of Spanish Studies: Twentieth Century* 6, no. 1 (1978):39–52. Good studies of "Chac Mool," "Tlactocatzine, del jardín de Flandes," and "Por boca de los dioses."

Yates, Donald A. "The Spanish American Detective Story." *Modern Language Journal,* 40, no. 5 (1956):228–32. Traces popularity of foreign writers such as Poe, Gaboriau, and Doyle; names few Latin American authors of genre, including literary detective stories of Borges and Bioy Casares.

General Anthologies in Spanish and Portuguese

Aguilera Malta, and Mejía Valera, Manuel. *El cuento actual latinoamericano.* Mexico City: Ediciones de Andrea, 1973.

Anderson Imbert, Enrique, and Florit, Eugenio. *Literatura hispanoamericana: Antología e introducción histórica.* New York: Holt, Rinehardt and Winston, 1960.

Anderson Imbert, Enrique, and Kiddle, Lawrence B. *Veinte cuentos hispanoamericanos del siglo XX.* New York: Appleton Century Crofts, 1956.

Batchelor, C. Malcolm. *Cuentos de acá y de allá.* Boston: Houghton Mifflin, 1953.

Battilana, Beatriz G. de, and Noriega, Néstor Alfredo. *17 cuentos hispanoamericanos.* Santa Fe, Argentina: Editorial APIS, 1974.

Bosi, Alfredo. *O conto brasileiro contemporaneo.* 2nd ed. Sao Paulo: Editora Cultrix, 1975.

Carilla, Emilio. *El cuento fantástico.* Buenos Aires: Editorial Nova, 1968.

Correas de Zapata, Celia C. de, and Johnson, Lygia. *Detrás de la reja. antología crítica de narradores latinoamericanas del siglo XX.* Caracas: Monte Avila, 1980.

Flores, Angel. *Historia y antología del cuento y la novela en Hispanoamérica.* New York: Las Américas Publishing Co., 1959.

Latcham, Ricardo. *Antología del cuento hispanoamericano contemporáneo.* Santiago: Zig-Zag, 1958.

Lida de Malkiel, María. *El cuento popular hispanoamericano y la literatura.* Buenos Aires: Facultad de Filosofía y Letras de la Universidad de Buenos Aires, 1941.

Manzor, Antonio R. *Antología del cuento hispanoamericano.* Santiago: Zig-Zag, 1940.

Menton, Seymour. *El cuento hispanoamericano: antología critico-histórica*. 2 vols. Mexico City: Fondo de Cultura Económica, 1970.

Mullen, Edward J., and Garganigo, John F. *El cuento hispánico: (A Graded Literary Anthology)*. New York: Random House, 1980.

Nazoa, Aquiles. *Cuentos contemporáneos hispanoamericanos*. La Paz, Bolivia: Ediciones Buriball, 1957.

Quijano, Aníbal. *Los mejores cuentos americanos*. Lima: Mejía Baca, (n.d.)

Sanz y Díaz, José. *Antología de cuentistas hispanoamericanos*. Madrid: Aguilar, 1946.

Vazquez, Alberto. *Cuentos de América española*. New York: Logmans, Green, 1952.

Yates, Donald A. *El cuento policial latinoamericano*. Mexico City: Ediciones de Andrea, 1964.

For an extensive listing of regional and national anthologies, consult the Leal and Menton works.

Selected Listing of Major Studies in Spanish and Portuguese

Alazraki, Jaime, et al. *El cuento hispanoamericano ante la crítica*. Madrid: Castalia, 1981.

———. *La prosa narrativa de Jorge Luis Borges*. Madrid: Editorial Gredos, 1968.

Aldana, Adelfo L. *La cuentística de Augusto Roa Bastos*. Montevideo: Ediciones Geminis, 1975.

Amícola, José. *Sobre Cortázar*. Buenos Aires: Editorial Escuela, 1969.

Anderson Imbert, Enrique. *La originalidad de Rubén Darío*. Buenos Aires: Centro Editor de América Latina, 1967.

Becco, Horacio Jorge. *Cuentistas argentinos*. Buenos Aires: Ministerio de Educación y Justicia, 1961.

Bratosevich, Nicolás A. S. *El estilo de Horacio Quiroga en sus cuentos*. Madrid. Gredos, 1973.

Cantonet, María. *Las vertientes de Javier de Viana*. Montevideo: Alfa, 1979.

Carter, Boyd G. *En torno a Gutiérrez Nájera*. Mexico City: Ediciones Botas, 1960.

Castañon Barrientos, Carlos. *El cuento modernista en Bolivia: estudio y antología*. La Paz: Empresa Editora Universo, 1972.

Castellanos, Luis A. *El cuento en la Argentina*. Rosario: Instituto Argentino de Cultura Hispánica de Rosario, 1967.

Cruz Castelán, Charlotte A. *Vista general del cuento-corto contemporánea de México y de los Estados Unidos de Nortéamerica*. Mexico City: Universidad Nacional Autónoma de México, 1956.

Fabbiani Ruiz, José. *El cuento en Venezuela*. Caracas: Pensamiento Vivo, 1953.

Ghiano, Juan Carlos. *El matadero de Echeverría y el costumbrismo*. Buenos Aires: Centro Editor de América Latina, 1968.

Girault Díaz Lombardo, María. *Consideraciones críticas sobre algunos cuentistas mexicanos.* Mexico City: 1957.

Gomes, Celuta Moreira. *O conto brasileiro e sua crítica. Bibliografia (1841– 1974).* Rio de Janeiro: Biblioteca Nacional, 1977.

González Lanuza, Eduardo. *Genio y figura de Roberto J. Payró.* Buenos Aires: Editorial Universitaria de Buenos Aires, 1965.

Jitrik, Noé. *Esteban Echeverría.* Buenos Aires: Centro Editor de América Latina, 1967.

Jurado, Alicia. *Genio y figura de Jorge Luis Borges.* Buenos Aires: Editorial Universidad de Buenos Aires, 1964.

Lagmanovich, David, ed. *Estudios sobre los cuentos de Julio Cortázar.* Barcelona: Ediciones Hispamérica, 1975.

Lancelotti, Mario A. *Teoría del cuento.* Buenos Aires: Ministerio de Cultura y Educación, Ediciones Culturales Argentinas, 1973.

Lanuza, José Luis. *Esteban Echeverría y sus amigos.* Buenos Aires: Paidós, 1967.

Leal, Luis. *Breve historia del cuento mexicano.* Mexico City. Studium, 1957; 2da edición, 1971.

————. *Historia del cuento hispanoamericano.* Mexico City: Studium, 1966.

Loveluck, Juan. *El cuento chileno (1864–1920).* Buenos Aires: Editorial Universitaria de Buenos Aires, 1964.

McAdam, Alfred. *El individuo y el otro: crítica a los cuentos de Julio Cortázar.* Buenos Aires: Ediciones La Librería, 1971.

Mancera Galletti, Angel. *Quienes narran y cuentan en Venezuela. Fichero bibliográfico para una historia de la novela y del cuento venezolanos.* Caracas: Ediciones Caribe, 1958.

Mastrángelo, Carlos. *El cuento argentino, contribución al conocimiento de su historia, teoría y práctica.* Buenos Aires: Editorial Nova, 1975.

Mejía Sánchez, Ernesto. *Los primeros cuentos de Rubén Darío.* Mexico City: Studium, 1951.

Meléndez, Concha. *El arte del cuento en Puerto Rico.* New York: Las Américas, 1961.

Menton, Seymour. *El cuento costarricense.* Mexico City: Ediciones de Andrea, 1964.

Miguel-Pereira, Lucía. *História da literatura brasileira; prosa de ficção—de 1970 a 1920.* 3rd ed. Rio de Janeiro: Livraria José Olympio Editora, 1973.

Moisés, Massaud, and Paes, José Paulo. *Pequeno dicionário de literatura brasileira.* 2nd ed. São Paulo: Editora Cultrix, 1980.

Montello, Josué. *O conto brasileiro: de Machado de Assis a Monteiro Lobato.* Rio de Janeiro: Edições de Ouro Culturais, 1967.

Nolasco, Sócrates. *El cuento en Santo Domingo.* Ciudad Trujillo: Librería Dominicano, 1957.

Orgambide, Pedro G. *Horacio Quiroga: El hombre y su obra.* Buenos Aires: Stilcograf, 1954.

Peralta Peralta, Jaime. *Cuentistas chileanos de la generación de 1950.* Madrid: Insula, 1963.

Perera, Hilda. *Idapo: El sincretismo en los cuentos negros de Lydia Cabrera.* Miami: Ediciones Universal, 1971.

Portuguez de Bolaños, Elizabeth. *El cuento en Costa Rica.* San José: A. Lehmann, 1964.

Pupo-Walker, Enrique, ed. *El cuento hispanoamericano ante la crítica.* Madrid: Castalia, 1973.

Rama, Angel. *Rubén Darío y el modernismo.* Caracas: Universidad Central de Venezuela, 1970.

Rivera-Rodas, Oscar. *La nueva narrativa boliviana: approximación a sus aspectos formales.* La Paz: Ediciones Camarlingi, 1972.

Rodríguez Alcalá, Hugo. *El arte de Juan Rulfo.* Mexico City: Instituto Nacional de Bellas Artes, Departamento de Literatura, 1975.

Rodríguez Monegal, Emir. *Genio y figura de Horacio Quiroga.* Buenos Aires: Editorial Universitaria, 1967.

Ruiz Vernaci, Enrique. *Introducción al cuento panameño y cuentos de Salomón Ponce Aguilera, Darío Herrera y Ricardo Miró.* Panamá: Biblioteca Selecta, 1946.

Silva Castro, Raúl. *Baldomero Lillo, 1867–1923.* Santiago: Nascimento, 1968.

Teutli Tayessier, M. *Aportación al estudio de los cuentistas de la revolución mexicana.* Mexico: Universidad Nacional Autónoma de México, 1956.

Tijeras, Eduardo. *Relato breve en Argentina.* Madrid: Cultura Hispánica, 1973.

INDEX